CULTURES OF THE WORLD
Moldova

Patricia Sheehan and Lynette Quek

mc **Marshall Cavendish**
Benchmark
New York

PICTURE CREDITS

Cover: © John McConnico/AP Photo
Alamy/Bes Stock: 30, 44 • Alamy/Photolibrary: 5, 10, 18, 21, 26, 27, 31, 50, 63, 81, 83, 86, 99, 102, 110, 111, 122, 124, 125, 126, 127, 129 • alt.type/Reuters: 32, 33, 34, 36, 38, 39, 119, 120 • Audrius Tomonis: 133 • Corbis Inc.: 22, 28, 35, 45, 70, 103, 104, 105, 108, 116 • Francis Tan: 130, 131 • Getty Images: 16, 17, 29, 49, 66, 93 • Lonely Planet Images: 98 • Photolibrary: 1, 11, 20, 23, 41, 42, 48, 77, 92, 109 • Spectrum Photofile: 89 • Valerii Corcimari: 3, 6, 7, 8, 9, 12, 13, 14, 15, 19, 24, 25, 40, 43, 46, 47, 51, 52, 53, 55, 56, 57, 59, 60, 61, 62, 64, 65, 67, 68, 69, 71, 72, 73, 74, 75, 76, 78, 79, 80, 82, 84, 85, 88, 90, 91, 94, 95, 96, 97, 100, 106, 112, 113, 114, 115, 117, 118, 121, 123, 128

PRECEDING PAGE

A horse stands amid the grass valleys of Moldova.

Publisher (U.S.): Michelle Bisson
Editors: Deborah Grahame, Mindy Pang
Copyreader: Sherry Chiger
Designers: Nancy Sabato, Benson Tan
Cover picture researcher: Connie Gardner
Picture researcher: Thomas Khoo

Marshall Cavendish Benchmark
99 White Plains Road
Tarrytown, NY 10591
Website: www.marshallcavendish.us

© Times Media Private Limited 2000
© Marshall Cavendish International (Asia) Private Limited 2011
® "Cultures of the World" is a registered trademark of Times Publishing Limited.

Originated and designed by Times Media Private Limited
An imprint of Marshall Cavendish International (Asia) Private Limited
A member of Times Publishing Limited

Marshall Cavendish is a trademark of Times Publishing Limited.

All Internet sites were correct and accurate at the time of printing. All monetary figures in this publication are in U.S. dollars.

Library of Congress Cataloging-in-Publication Data
Sheehan, Patricia, 1954-.
  Moldova / Patricia Sheehan and Lynette Quek. — 2nd ed.
      p. cm. — (Cultures of the world)
  Summary: "Provides comprehensive information on the geography, history,
    wildlife, governmental structure, economy, cultural diversity, peoples,
    religion, and culture of Moldova"—Provided by publisher.
  Includes bibliographical references and index.
  ISBN 978-1-60870-025-7
  1. Moldova—Juvenile literature. I. Quek, Lynette. II. Title.
  DK509.56.S53 2010
  947.6—dc22   2010001208

Printed in China
7 6 5 4 3 2 1

CONTENTS

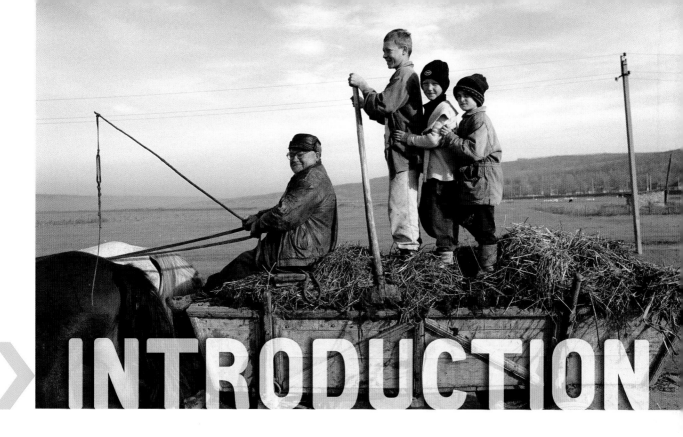

INTRODUCTION

MOLDOVA IS NOT A COUNTRY THAT FIGURES MUCH IN THE European imagination. Anonymous to the world and tucked away in southeast Europe, Moldova is nestled between Ukraine in the north, the east, and the south and Romania in the west. Communism ruled this former Soviet republic for 51 years, forever changing the lives of millions, until the Soviet Union collapsed in 1991. The collapse brought economic decline and instability to Moldova, and in 2001, angry citizens backed the return of the Communists. But the country has remained desperately poor. In April 2009, more than 10,000 young Moldovans protested against the country's Communist leadership, desperate to escape the Soviet time warp and join Western Europe. After nearly two decades of independence, Moldovans are still at odds over the question of who they are. In spite of the country's troubles, its people have remained resilient through centuries of struggle. Those who visit the country are struck by the warmth of its people and its distinctive multiethnic character. Moldovan life today continues to embody a love of family, the land and its pleasures, and a desire to modernize and integrate into larger European society.

GEOGRAPHY

Azure blue waters and terraced farmlands weave through the landscape of Moldova.

MOLDOVA IS A SMALL LANDLOCKED country slightly larger than Maryland. Located between the Prut and Dniester rivers, it measures 217 miles (350 km) long and 93 miles (150 km) wide, covering around 13,070 square miles (33,851 square km). Moldova shares 279 miles (449 km) of border with Romania in the west and 583 miles (938 km) of border with Ukraine in the north, the east, and the south.

A village in the Orhei district. One third of Moldova is covered by plains and fluvial terraces.

PHYSICAL ENVIRONMENT

Moldova is an extremely fertile land with an average elevation of 482 feet (147 m) above sea level. Its highest point, Mount Balanesti, stands at 1,411 feet (430 m). The country's topography is diverse, ranging gently from rolling, hilly plain in the north to deciduous forests and mountainous highlands in the center to a steppe zone in the south.

RIVERS

There are approximately 3,000 rivers and streams in Moldova, and all of them drain south to the Black Sea. Only 246 exceed 6 miles (10 km) in length; just eight extend more than 62 miles (100 km). Three river valleys running from northwest to southeast contain most of Moldova's towns.

To the east, the Dniester forms part of the border with Ukraine and is navigable almost throughout the country. The Dniester drains an area of about 30,000 square miles (77,700 square km) and is an important traffic artery for the shipment of grain, vegetables, sunflower seeds, cattle and cattle products, and lumber. All these crops are produced in the Dniester Basin. The Dniester swells during the rainy season and at the end of winter, when the ice starts to melt. If the winter is warm, however, the river does not freeze.

The Raut, a short tributary of the Dniester, flows within a narrow valley in central Moldova. In the west, the Prut River divides Moldova from Romania. It

The Raut River on a hot summer afternoon.

is a tributary of the Danube, which it joins at the southern tip of the country. The Ialpug, the Cogalnic, and other southern rivers flow into the estuary of the Danube River in nearby Ukraine.

There are 2,200 natural springs in Moldova. They are tapped for the country's water supply.

CLIMATE AND SEASONS

The country has a temperate continental climate. Average daily temperatures in the summer generally exceed 67°F (19°C). Winters are mild, with average daily temperatures ranging from 23°F to 27°F (-5°C to -3°C).

Conditions in the fall are changeable, with heavy rains in some years and droughts in others. Rain is heaviest in the higher regions, where it can exceed 21.7 inches (55 cm) per year. In the south, annual average precipitation is 15.7 inches (40 cm). Of the past 110 years, 43 were drought years.

Wintertime in Moldova sees the shrubs and mountains clad in soft white snow.

FLORA

About 2,000 plant species and an additional 3,000 species of mosses, fungi, lichens, and algae can be found in Moldova. They grow primarily in the northern and eastern parts of the country. However, many of these species are decreasing, and habitats for animals are becoming increasingly scarce as a result of intensive land use for agriculture and the destruction of wetlands for urban development.

Moldovan forests have the highest proportion of broad-leaved species of any temperate zone country. Oak trees are the predominant genus, occupying 52 percent of total land area. The second most common genus, *Robinia*, was introduced to stabilize poor soils. It can survive in polluted soil and thus prevents erosion. Other common types of tree include ash, beech, and hornbeam. Forests of hornbeam used to be found in more than a third of Moldova, but now they can only be found in the central part of the country. Ash trees are found almost everywhere in the country, as are maple trees. Other flora include linden and wild pear.

Evening sets in the valley as the sun recedes behind the hills at a forest in Moldova.

FAUNA

Many kinds of fauna flourish in Moldova. The country has 15,000 animal species, 109 of which are endangered. On the steppes, hamsters, hares, and partridges are predominant. The forest steppe is populated by wild boars, badgers, and wolves, among other animals.

Of all deer species, the roe deer is the most common. Many other species of deer are no longer found in Moldova. To curb the declining numbers, some animal species have been introduced to the country. For example, the Kashmir deer was a local species that almost disappeared in the 1950s. Since then the Ascanian deer has been introduced to the Moldovan forests and reserves, as have the European elk and the Sika deer. Other imported species include the Siberian stag, the fallow deer, and the muskrat.

There are a rich variety of birds, both resident and migratory. Commonly found species include the hawk, the woodlark, and the long-eared owl. Along the rivers, ducks, wild geese, and herons can be seen.

The dwindling fish population is of great concern to environmentalists. Among the 75 species, the most common are perch, pike, bream, and roach. Some species, such as trout, are no longer found in Moldova.

A roe deer and her fawn roam freely at a nature reserve in Moldova.

Some of the most severe cases of soil pollution take place in river valleys, such as in the Raut Valley (*above*).

ENVIRONMENTAL ISSUES

SOIL POLLUTION During the five decades of Soviet leadership, Moldova's agricultural land was heavily worked to produce cheap goods for the Soviet Union. Creation of new agricultural lands, careless cultivation, and the discharge of manure and other types of untreated animal waste have all led to soil degradation.

The greatest pollution comes from excessive fertilization. The use of chemical fertilizers per acre has increased from year to year. By 1990, 25 percent of the food produced was polluted with nitrates. The Agricultural Pollution Control Project (APCP), which plans to educate farmers on sustainable practices in crop and livestock production, aims to reduce this dependence on chemicals.

WATER POLLUTION Almost 28 percent of the total population depends on surface water in Moldova, while the rest of the population consumes underground water. Almost 8 percent of the water comes from aquifers, and only half of the water meets drinking standards. Many of the rural wells are either drying up or contaminated with minerals and bacteria. Most of the river valleys and lake areas are in use for agricultural production, and Moldova has no system to remove chemicals and salt from the polluted water. Moldova also lacks almost any source of chemically cleaned drinking water that is within the admissible standards of hygiene.

Supported by Global Environment Facility (GEF) funding of US$10.74 million, Moldova has taken on a project to reduce pollution from its agricultural sources draining out to the Danube River and the Black Sea. The APCP will help the government to adopt environmentally friendly practices in crop and livestock production; strengthen national policy as well as regulatory and institutional capacity to control agricultural pollution; and increase public awareness of environmental degradation.

Nutrient runoff control is particularly important to Moldova, as about 34 percent of the country drains into the Prut River, a tributary of the Danube; approximately 60 percent into the Dniester River; and the rest into small rivers that empty out into the Black Sea. Agricultural pollution, together with overfishing, mismanagement of game sources, poaching, draining of wetlands for crop cultivation, and illegal tree cutting (right), has led to a reduction in biodiversity, which has reached alarming levels in the lower Prut River Basin. Native flora and fauna species are severely threatened, and some even face extinction.

AIR POLLUTION Under the Soviets, pollution controls were not installed, and emissions from factories in neighboring republics drifted over Moldova. Today polluted air is mostly found in Balti, Rabnita, Chisinau, and Tiraspol, and three-quarters of it is caused by cars. High concentrations of formaldehyde, a volatile, probably carcinogenic toxin, have been discovered in Balti and Chisinau, where levels have reached four times the maximum permissible concentration. Since the Chernobyl disaster in 1986, where a flawed radioactive reactor design operated by inadequately trained personnel blew up and resulted in widespread radiation poisoning, local power plants have stepped up their vigilance. Radioactive waste was buried in this region, and a few accidents in the past have added to the contamination. To keep radiation at bay, Moldova's government stipulated that the maximum permissible concentration of formaldehyde be contained at a safe level of 3 mcg/m3.

CITIES

The republic is divided into 32 districts, three municipalities (Balti, Chisinau, and Tighina), one autonomous territorial unit (Gagauzia), and another, nonautonomous territorial unit (Transnistria). Moldova has around 65 cities and towns and more than 1,575 villages. The major cities include the capital city, Chisinau (formerly spelled Kishinev), with 712,218 people; Tiraspol, with 184,000; Balti, with 162,000; and Tighina, with 132,000.

CHISINAU Founded in 1420, Chisinau lies on the Ikel River in the center of Moldova. It grew rapidly from a small village into an important rail junction

One of the major causes of air pollution is the increasing number of cars on the roads as urban Moldovans become more affluent.

between Romania and Russia during the 19th century. Chisinau suffered massive destruction during World War II, when bombing and fighting destroyed more than 70 percent of the buildings. Most of the existing buildings date from the mid-20th century, when the city was rebuilt. Main streets were widened, tall office buildings were constructed, and industrial parks were planned. Factories in the suburbs account for nearly half of all industrial production in Moldova.

Many shops are found in the capital, as shopping is a major recreational pursuit. The city looks like a typical Soviet provincial city—built on a rectangular grid with huge concrete, nondescript buildings. Along the main street, the monotony is broken with some neoclassical mansions—a reminder of the country's past. Since independence, the main street, formerly named Lenina after Lenin, has been renamed Stefan cel Mare Boulevard. Many other streets have also been renamed, in most instances to honor Romanians instead of Soviet figures. Piata Marii Adunari Nationale, the main square, has a triumphal arch built in 1846. Behind it is a huge cathedral, recently restored, and a park with a section reserved for statues from the classics of Romanian literature.

The city is the center of arts in the country. It has numerous museums, such as the National Art Museum, the National History Museum, and the Archaeology Museum, theaters, and an opera house. A beautiful lake runs along the central park of the city, which is located near the state university. One of the city's most beautiful buildings is the Ciuflea Church. It has majestic, sky-blue towers, and each of the icons inside the church is decorated with a different frame.

TIRASPOL, the second-largest city in Moldova, is located east of Tighina on the Dniester River. Tiraspol was founded in 1792. Like other cities, it faced heavy destruction during battles between the Soviet Union and Germany. Today it is the capital of the self-proclaimed republic Transnistria. Its population consists mainly of Russians, ethnic Moldovans, and ethnic Ukrainians.

Tiraspol is now an industrial center well known for canning and winemaking. Other industries in Tiraspol produce farm equipment, footwear, textiles, furniture, and carpets.

The Sheriff Stadium of Tiraspol, located in the Transnistrian region of Moldova. Tiraspol is the second-largest city in Moldova and is the capital and administrative center of the de facto independent Pridnestrovian Moldavian Republic (Transnistria).

BALTI lies on the Raut River and is the largest city in the north. It is home to several of Moldova's major industries, such as winemaking, sugar refining, and tobacco processing. Fur coats, machinery, and furniture are also manufactured here.

TIGHINA is one of the country's oldest cities, founded around the second century B.C. Its Russian name is Bender, which means "belonging to the Turks." Tighina is situated southeast of Chisinau on the right bank of the Dniester River. Throughout history, the city has been attacked and occupied by numerous foreign powers. It has also been rebuilt many times following destruction in various violent clashes. In 1992 it was the center of fighting between ethnic Russians and the Moldovan military. Today it is where Russian-led peacekeeping forces in the region live.

Tighina is a manufacturing center for textiles, electrical equipment, and food. Silk made in Tighina is among the finest in the world. A 17th-century Turkish fortress still stands in the city as a reminder of the turbulent past.

A triumphal arch seen in Bender, or Tighina, the fourth-largest city in Moldova, also located in the Transnistrian region.

HISTORY

The Victory Memorial Monument at Eternitate Memorial Complex is dedicated to Moldovans who fought during World War II.

THROUGHOUT HISTORY, MOLDOVA has been subject to frequent invasions and foreign domination. Each era left a legacy, but Moldova has been influenced mostly by the Soviet Union. The imperial and Soviet governments tried to integrate Moldova's economy into their own and Russianize the Moldovan people.

For a long time that plan seemed to work, but in 1991 Moldova declared independence and went its separate way. Independence was not a new experience for the country, as it had existed briefly as a sovereign state before, but this time there was much to undo from the previous regime.

Transnistrian people asking for Russian support in a demonstration.

EARLY HISTORY

The Dacians were the ancestors of the Moldovans. Numerous archaeological traces have been found, including burial places and religious cult constructions between the Dniester and Prut rivers, dating to the fourth century B.C. Farmers who settled in the river valleys, the Dacians traded with the Greeks, who had established trading posts along the Black Sea coast.

The Romans conquered the Dacians in the third and second centuries A.D., and the local population had to learn Latin. The Romans built roads, forts, and trading centers but eventually left the area for conquests farther afield. Slavs settled in their wake. About this time the Romanian language developed from Latin. Various nobles ruled the area, and one of them, Bogdan of Cuhea, founded the principality of Moldavia, which included the area known as Bessarabia (eastern Moldova). The first document referring to the land of Moldavia dates to A.D. 1360. In 1391, ethnic Moldavians were mentioned for the first time.

The majestic Fortress of Soroca on the bank of the Dniester River.

MOLDAVIA AND THE TURKS

The most important figure to the formation of the medieval Moldavian state was Stephen the Great (c. 1433—1504), who defended Moldavia's sovereignty in battles with the Turks, the Hungarians, the Polish royal troops, and the Crimean khans. Fortresses from his time still stand. The medieval principality was, for much of its history, under Austro-Hungarian rule. A large part of Moldavia was later incorporated into present-day Romania and Ukraine.

During his rule, Stephen organized a strong force of peasants to resist the Turkish sultan. His efforts were successful, and on August 20, 1503, he finally signed a treaty with the sultan that managed to preserve Moldavia's independence, at the cost of an annual tribute to the Turks. Stephen was also a supporter of the arts and a religious crusader, and his architects built Orthodox churches throughout the country. In addition he increased trade links with the rest of Europe and the Middle East.

After Stephen's death, Moldavia became part of the Turkish Empire in 1513 and remained so for the next 300 years. This was a stable period, but by the 18th century, the empire began to break up. Between 1711 and 1812, the Russians gained control of Moldavia five times. Eventually Turkey was defeated by Russia. As a result of the Treaty of Bucharest in 1812, which ended the Russo-Turkish War, Moldavia became part of the Russian Empire. But this did not last very long. By the beginning of the 20th century, western Moldavia had become part of the united nation of Romania. Bessarabia, in the eastern part of Moldavia, remained under Russian control.

A monument to Stephen the Great, hero in the hearts of many Moldovans. Many streets in Moldova are named after him.

WORLD WARS

During World War I, Russia suffered great damage. There were widespread food shortages, and people became disillusioned with the empire. Following the Bolshevik Revolution in 1917, the Russian Empire collapsed, a year before World War I ended. Bessarabia declared independence from Russia and united with Romania. A treaty was signed on October 20, 1920.

In 1922 the Russian Communist leaders founded the Union of Soviet Socialist Republics (USSR), which included Russia, Ukraine, and several nearby republics. In 1939 the USSR (led by Stalin) and Germany (led by Hitler) signed a treaty that banned hostilities between the two countries and allowed Stalin to annex territory. A year later the USSR occupied Bessarabia and renamed it the Moldavian Soviet Socialist Republic.

When World War II began, the USSR had to defend itself against Germany, despite their nonaggression pact. Romania, allied with Germany, attacked Ukraine and reoccupied Soviet Moldavia from 1941 to 1944 until Soviet forces retook the territory.

This memorial in Chisinau remembers the pioneers who lost their lives during World War I.

SOVIET RULE

With the restoration of Soviet rule in 1944, Moldavia was subjected to large-scale immigration of Russians and Ukrainians, especially to the industrial centers along the eastern bank of the Dniester. Stalin decided that Moldavians and Romanians were now separate ethnic groups, even though the former had relatives across the Prut River in Romania. He insisted that the language the Moldavians spoke was not Romanian but Moldavian, and he imposed the Cyrillic alphabet used by Russians to replace the Latin alphabet used by Romanians. Russian became the official language.

In 1950 Leonid Brezhnev, a Soviet official from Ukraine, was sent to Moldavia to ensure compliance with Soviet laws. Private farms were declared Soviet property, and government-run farms were worked under the direction of Russian and Ukrainian managers. During the 1970s and 1980s, after becoming president of the USSR, Brezhnev continued the policy of Russianization. The Soviet government closed churches and synagogues, and more ethnic Russians and Ukrainians began to settle in Moldavia.

STRIVING FOR INDEPENDENCE

Moldova's gradual movement to independence sped up in 1986 with Soviet leader Mikhail Gorbachev's reformist regime and policy of glasnost, which means "openness" in Russian. As the Soviet Union started to relax its policies, a number of independent political groups in Moldova evolved, working toward national and cultural independence. The Popular Front of Moldavia was formed, and pro-independence pressure, often supported by mass demonstrations, intensified.

A former Soviet combatant proudly displays his Soviet military distinctions.

The leaders of Soviet Moldavia agreed to some demands, such as the use of Moldovan as the official language, and Romanian names replaced Russian names for major cities. Moldova's progress toward independence and reform accelerated after economist Mircea Druc was appointed prime minister in May 1990. In June 1990 the Moldavian parliament changed the republic's name to Moldova, adopted the blue, yellow, and red colors of Romania's flag, and issued a declaration of sovereignty. The following summer 100,000 Moldovans took to the streets demanding independence, and Gorbachev could do little to stop Moldova from leaving the Soviet Union.

AFTER INDEPENDENCE

On August 27, 1991, the Republic of Moldova officially gained its independence and became a sovereign state. The move was followed by the establishment

Mircea Snegur, the first president of Moldova, saluting his people after winning the elections of 1991.

of customs posts on the border with Ukraine. A Moldovan national army was also formed.

The first presidential elections were held in December 1991, and Mircea Snegur was elected president. Multiparty parliamentary elections were held in February 1994, and the Communist-led Agrarian Democratic Party won the largest number of seats. A bloc of socialist parties came in second. Petru Lucinschi was elected speaker of the parliament, and the government was headed by Prime Minister Andrei Sangheli. The parliament passed a new constitution for the Republic of Moldova, and in April 1995 the first multiparty elections were held for local, self-governing bodies. Presidential elections were held again in 1996, where Lucinschi won a surprise victory over the incumbent Snegur, to became the country's second president.

President Lucinschi did manage to institute some very controversial reforms. (Perhaps the United States Assistance for International Development-funded "Pamînt" land privatization program was the most controversial.) Indeed, his tenure was marked by constant legislative struggles with Moldova's parliament. Several times, the parliament considered votes of no confidence in the president's government, and a succession of moderate, pro-Western reform prime ministers were dismissed by a parliament that increasingly favored the growing Communist Party faction.

At the legislative elections in 1998, the Party of Communists of the Republic of Moldova, which was relegalized in 1994 after being banned in 1991, was reduced to opposition when an Alliance for Democracy and Reforms was formed. However, the ensuing governments were marked by chronic political instability, which led to the alliance's disintegration and an overwhelming Party of Communists victory in the 2001 and 2005 elections, instating Vladimir Voronin as president. Although the Communists gained the majority of the vote again during the 2009 elections, the other four parties combined secured a greater percentage of the parliament, which led to the formation of a coalition called the Alliance for European Integration.

SEPARATIST MOVEMENTS

The single most important political challenge facing Moldova after gaining independence was resistance to Moldovan rule and a move toward separatism on the part of two ethnic minorities. The first group lives on the eastern side of the Dniester, in a region known as Transnistria, and is led by ethnic Russians. The second group, in the south of the country, is led by members of the Gagauz, a Christian, Turkic ethnic group.

Moldovans sit by their tents during a strike.

When Moldova became independent, these two groups were concerned about their future and the protection of their national and ethnic status. These concerns were based on fears that Moldova would unite with Romania, as regions of Moldova had historically been part of Romania. These fears were exacerbated when Moldovan became the official language of Moldova, although Russian was permitted for interethnic communication. Russian speakers marched through the capital and walked off their jobs to protest what they viewed as increased discrimination. Their displeasure remains today.

TRANSNISTRIA SEPARATISTS

Tensions between ethnic Romanians and ethnic Russians worsened in 1990. Local officials refused to enact the language law in the area east of Transnistria, where large numbers of Slavs reside but do not constitute a majority of the population. A political group promoting greater autonomy for the area was formed. On September 2, 1990, Transnistria separatists declared the region an Autonomous Soviet Socialist Republic, but the Moldovan parliament immediately annulled the declaration. Violence erupted in November 1990 during elections for representatives to the Transnistria Supreme Soviet. The

A sculpture in the Eternitate Memorial Complex in Chisinau was built in 1992 to honor the people who perished during the years of the Transdniestrian War.

conflict escalated in late 1991 when, following Moldova's declaration of independence from the Soviet Union, the leaders of the Transnistria separatists declared the region's independence from Moldova. Fighting in the spring of 1992 resulted in many lives lost and considerable damage to the economies of both Transnistria and Moldova.

A cease-fire was declared in July 1992, and the Russian 14th Army, based in the Transnistrian region prior to Moldovan independence, acted as peacekeepers. To prevent further bloodshed, the Moldovan and Russian prime ministers later signed a withdrawal treaty.

In 1995 the Russian president, Boris Yeltsin, acknowledged Moldova's territorial integrity, and the issue of Transnistria's sovereignty returned to the negotiating table. A signed accord guaranteed Transnistria's autonomy, but independence was not granted. Nevertheless, Transnistria took matters into its own hands and held elections in December 1995, much to the displeasure of the Moldovan government. Igor Smirnov was elected president of the region.

In May 1997 a memorandum recognizing Moldova's territorial authority over Transnistria was signed in Moscow. Discussions commenced for the drafting of a final document to govern the normalization of relations between Moldova and the Transnistria separatists. Yeltsin indicated that Russian troops would stay in the region until a settlement was reached.

GAGAUZ SEPARATISTS

The Gagauz enjoy local autonomy in the southern part of the country. In August 1990 they proclaimed their region to be an Autonomous Soviet

Socialist Republic, but the Moldovan parliament did not recognize it. The 1994 Moldovan elections marked the turning point in relations between the Moldovan government and Gagauz representatives. One particularly important issue for the Gagauz was the abolition of the 1989 language law, which made Moldovan the only official language. As the majority of the Gagauz are not fluent in Moldovan, they are afraid that they will lose their influence in the country.

A new law has since designated Moldovan, Gaugauzian, and Russian as the three official languages. The Moldovan parliament also ratified the Gagauz region's special status. Under Moldovan law, the region remains part of Moldovan territory, and the Moldovan government determines its budget. A locally elected parliamentary assembly, governor, and executive committee act as the local government. In elections for the executive committee and parliamentary assembly, held in the spring and summer of 1995, the Communist Party gained the largest number of seats.

COMMONWEALTH OF INDEPENDENT STATES

In 1992 Moldova joined the Commonwealth of Independent States (CIS), an alliance of former Soviet republics, and gained a seat in the United Nations. The alliance with CIS helped Moldova acquire raw materials and provide a market for its finished goods, which is necessary now that the Soviet Union has ceased to exist. There is constant tension between conservatives in the country who want to return to the old days of central control and liberals who want a restructured market economy. The strained relations between Moldovans and ethnic Russians and Turks in their autonomous areas continue, and while Russian troops remain in Transnistria, this will remain a serious issue.

A statue of Lenin stands impressively at Comrat in the Autonomous Territorial Unit of Gagauzia.

GOVERNMENT

A general view of the third congress of the
Moldova Liberal Democratic Party, held at
the National Palace in Chisinau in 2008.

THE COLLAPSE OF the Soviet Union in 1991 brought great benefits to much of Eastern Europe, but in Moldova it ushered in economic decline and instability. Moldova has worked hard ever since to establish democratic political systems, but changing from a Communist government to a democracy has been difficult.

The country remained desperately poor, and young people flocked overseas to work. There was a strong expectation of change, but that did not happen.

Under the Soviet system, the legislative branch of government was called the Supreme Soviet. On May 23, 1991, the Moldovan Supreme Soviet renamed itself the Parliament of the Republic of Moldova, which subsequently declared its independence from the Soviet Union.

Demonstrators gathered in Chisinau to protest against the results of a parliamentary election which the ruling Communist Party had won.

CONSTITUTIONAL DIVISION OF POWER

The new constitution of Moldova, passed by the national parliament on July 29, 1994, defines Moldova as a sovereign state with a free-market economy based on protection of private property rights and independent executive, legislative, and judicial branches of government.

Personal rights and freedoms are ensured according to the UN Universal Declaration of Human Rights. All citizens are equal before the law, regardless of ethnicity, language, religion, or political beliefs. The state guarantees the rights of political parties and other public organizations. In keeping with the country's ethnic and cultural diversity, the constitution enshrines the rights of all minorities and the autonomous status of the Transnistria and Gagauz regions. Administration of the cities and municipalities is based on the principles of local autonomy and democratic elections.

A soldier stands guard on the steps of the parliament.

GOVERNMENT INSTITUTIONS

THE EXECUTIVE BRANCH consists of the president (head of state), the prime minister (head of government), and a cabinet. The president is elected in a national election for a term of four years. He has broad powers and acts as the head of the military, with the authority to declare a state of military emergency, subject to parliamentary approval.

The president appoints a prime minister with the consent of parliament. He leads a Council of Ministers that carries out the functions of government. The president must be over 35 years old, a resident in Moldova for at least 10 years, and a speaker of Moldovan.

THE LEGISLATIVE BRANCH consists of a directly elected parliament. The parliament's 101 members are elected from party lists on a proportional representation basis. The most common reason given for the use of the party list/proportional representation (PL/PR) system is that the conflict over the

Transnistria region makes it impossible to have any single-member districts in the country. Each parliament sits for four years and has the power to adopt laws, approve the state budget, determine military matters, and exercise certain supervisory powers over the work of the government.

The Parliament of the Republic of Moldova (*Parlamentul Republicii Moldova*).

THE JUDICIAL BRANCH is a three-tier system that is independent of the executive and legislative branches. Municipal and district courts are generally courts of first instance, with appeals first to an appellate court and then ultimately to the Supreme Court, the highest court in Moldova. There are also specialized courts with jurisdiction over economic and military disputes. A constitutional court, which is independent of other courts, has jurisdiction over all matters relating to the interpretation of the provisions of the Moldovan constitution. Judges for the lower courts are appointed by the president for an initial period of five years. They may be reappointed for a subsequent 10 years. Supreme Court judges are appointed by the parliament for terms of not less than 15 years.

NATIONAL SECURITY

Armed forces are under the jurisdiction of the Ministry of Defense. In 1995 ground forces totaled about 11,000 and air force personnel about 1,300. There are 100,000 reservists, who had military service in the previous five years. Military units for the army consist of three motor rifle brigades, one artillery brigade, and one reconnaissance or assault battalion. The air force has one fighter regiment, one helicopter squadron, and one missile brigade. Military equipment includes arms from former Soviet stocks and undetermined quantities of arms from Romania. Internal security is provided by 2,500 national policemen and a riot police force of 900 personnel under the Ministry of Internal Affairs. The Russian 14th Army, acting as peacekeepers in Moldova, has a total force of 14,200. Guarding the Transnistrian region are the Cossacks, the armed forces of the self-proclaimed republic.

Riot policemen on duty during a protest in Chisinau.

POLITICAL PARTIES

A standoff between pro-Europe (ruling coalition) and pro-Russia (Communist Party) forces has long split Moldovan politics. Upon coming to power in July 2009, leaders of the ruling coalition promised renewed efforts to reach out to and cooperate with the Communists, who are now the opposition party after 10 years of control of parliament and the presidency.

Many were surprised when youths took control of Chisinau's main square, PiataMarii Adunari Nationale, in April 2009. The young Moldovans protested against the Communist-controlled government's way of conducting parliamentary elections. Pleas to major news networks to report on what was happening were ignored. Instead, the protesting youths used new media and social networking websites to thrust their country into the spotlight.

The youths, mostly students, succeeded in forcing the ruling Communist Party to admit that the parliamentary elections were neither free nor fair and to adjust the results in favor of the opposition. They paid a high price for this success, as at least three protesters were killed and scores were injured in connection with the uprising.

Moldovan nationalists and students at a protest rally in Chisinau to try to overthrow the Communist government.

The protests produced a chain of events that led to repeat parliamentary elections on July 29 that brought to power a four-party, Western-leaning, pro-reform coalition called the Alliance for European Integration (AEI). But the alliance controls only 53 seats in the 101-seat parliament, making it impossible for the coalition to elect a new president without at least eight votes from the now-opposition Communist faction.

RECENT ELECTIONS

Widespread dissatisfaction with largely ineffectual post-Soviet reformist governments and economic hardship saw angry citizens backing the return of the Communists and their social programs. In 2001 more than half of Moldova's voters cast their ballots for the Communist Party in the parliamentary elections. The parliament then elected the leader of the Communist faction, Vladimir Voronin, to be president on April 4. The Communist Party won the elections again in March 2005.

Moldovan citizens, including local policemen, wait to cast their ballots at a polling station.

Moldova's voters took part in two parliamentary elections in 2009. The first, in April, saw the Communists win, allegedly by government vote-rigging. This led to mass riots and protests, which in turn resulted in repeat elections in July. The central-right opposition coalition of the Liberal Democratic Party, the Liberal Party, the Democratic Party, and the Our Moldova Alliance won 50.7 percent of votes compared with 45.1 percent for the Communists, ending almost a decade of Communist rule. Outgoing president Voronin stepped down on September 11, 2009, after serving two terms. In his place Mihai Ghimpu became the acting president until the parliament elects a new president.

Members of the Liberal Democratic Party in Moldova at a political rally.

INTERNATIONAL RELATIONS

Since Moldova gained independence on August 27, 1991, many foreign countries have officially recognized its independent status. This is a very encouraging sign for the infant nation. Currently Moldova maintains diplomatic relations with 109 countries. Moldova is also a member of the United Nations (UN), the North Atlantic Cooperation Council, the European Bank for Reconstruction and Development, the World Bank, and the International Monetary Fund (IMF). On July 13, 1995, Moldova became the first former Soviet republic to be admitted to the Council of Europe.

With the assistance of the United Nations Development Program (UNDP), programs in democracy, entrepreneurship, supporting women in development, foreign trade, disaster mitigation, and sustainable human development were efficiently initiated. In addition, Moldova is a member of the North Atlantic Treaty Organization (NATO) Partnership for Peace program, the World Trade Organization, and the Organization for Security and Cooperation in Europe (OSCE).

The past few years have seen significant developments in Moldova's relations with the West. On February 22, 2005, Brussels and Chisinau signed an agreement on the EU (European Union)-Moldova Action Plan, a roadmap of reforms to strengthen the democratic and economic situation of the country and facilitate its Euro-Atlantic integration. In accordance with the plan, Moldova has begun to harmonize its laws with those of the EU. It has worked with the EU to crack down on smuggling, strengthen customs procedures, and facilitate cross-border cooperation along its Ukrainian border. In 2005 the EU dispatched a Border Assistance Mission to help stem the flow of illegal trade between Ukraine and Moldova.

Vladimir Voronin (*center*) at the Commonwealth of Independent States (CIS) summit in Moscow.

Moldova and other former Soviet republics make up the CIS, which promotes cooperation among its members. In September 1993 an agreement establishing the CIS Charter on Economic Union was signed by all CIS countries, including Moldova. In addition, the country has entered into agreements on the creation of a free-trade zone and a payment union with Russia and a number of other CIS countries.

In 2006 the U.S. Millennium Challenge Corporation (MCC) approved Moldova's $2.4 million Threshold Country Plan to combat corruption. Two years later, in November 2008, MCC and the government of Moldova signed an agreement to move forward with feasibility studies to determine how best to proceed with proposed road rehabilitation and agricultural projects. These studies will help ensure that the projects proposed by Moldova will significantly contribute to economic development and poverty reduction.

In the atmosphere of heightened international sensitivity to terrorism following the events of September 11, 2001, Moldova has been a supporter of American efforts to increase international cooperation in combating terrorism. Moldova has sent demining units and peacekeepers to participate in postconflict humanitarian assistance in Iraq.

TRANSNISTRIAN CONFLICT

Moldova remains divided, with separatist forces controlling Transnistria along the Ukrainian border. Transnistria is in reality separated politically and institutionally from the rest of the country. Moldova has a population of 4.7 million, 533,000 of whom live in Transnistria, Moldova's most industrialized region. Approximately 40 percent of the population of Transnistria is Romanian/Moldovan, 28 percent Ukrainian, and 23 percent Russian. The separatists have continually demanded "statehood" and recognition of Moldova as a confederation of two equal states.

The conflict between the Gagauz and Moldovans was kept below the level of large-scale violence, whereas the Transnistrian conflict escalated into full-fledged civil war in spring 1992. More than 1,000 people were said to have been killed, and more than 100,000 people had to flee their homes. Although this conflict had a strong ethnic component, it was not ethnic by nature; it

Above: Moldovan opposition leaders (*from left to right*) Mihai Ghimpu, Serafim Urecheanu and Vlad Filat, speak to the public at a conference.

Right: Vladimir Voronin was the third president of Moldova from 2001 until 2009 and leader of the Communist Party in Moldova.

was fought between the pro-independence political elite in Chisinau and the conservative pro-Soviet forces in Tiraspol. Moldovans and non-Moldovans could be found on both sides. The dispute has strained Moldova's relations with Russia, which in the past has cut energy supplies to Moldova, as well as banned wine imports from the country.

The July 1992 cease-fire agreement established a tripartite peacekeeping force consisting of Moldovan, Russian, and Transnistrian units. Mediators in the Transnistrian settlement negotiations representing Russia and Ukraine drafted an agreement in 1999 that recognizes Moldova as an independent, sovereign state and defines Transnistria as an autonomous republic within the Republic of Moldova. Transnistria would have its own state symbols—flag, emblem, anthem—and Moldovan, Ukrainian, and Russian as its three official languages. The mediators urged all sides to continue the peacekeeping operations in Transnistria with the added participation of Ukrainian peacekeepers.

Both sides have realized that without a solution to the status of Transnistria, all economic and social problems will be extremely difficult to solve.

Negotiations to resolve the conflict continue today, and the cease-fire is still in effect. Over the years, settlement talks have alternated between periods of forward momentum and periods of no progress. In 2003 the Moldovan government and Transnistrian authorities agreed to draft a constitution for a reintegrated state. Disagreements over the division of powers remained, however, and a settlement proved elusive. After a 15-month break, the sides met for a renewed round of negotiations in 2005. Mediators from Ukraine, Russia, and the OSCE joined Moldovan and Transnistrian representatives at

ACTING PRESIDENT

Born on November 19, 1951, in Chisinau and a lawyer by profession, Mihai Ghimpu was one of the founders of Moldova's pro-independence Popular Front in 1988 and served as a member of parliament from 1990 to 1998. He went on to help form and then lead the Liberal Party and was elected to the city council in Chisinau in 2007. His nephew Dorin Chirtoaca, the vice president of the Liberal Party, has been mayor of Chisinau since 2007 and played a leading role in opposing the governing Communist Party in the two parliamentary elections of 2009.

Mihai Ghimpu was once again elected to parliament in April 2009 and became speaker after the July election, when the anti-Communist opposition formed a new government. When Communist president Vladimir Voronin resigned on September 11, 2009, Ghimpu succeeded him on an acting basis until parliament elects a new president.

the talks. Little progress was made on a settlement, though, or on withdrawal of Russian troops from Transnistria.

Informal discussions held in Ukraine in April 2008 and in Moldova in July 2008 focused on creating favorable conditions for resumption of formal talks. In 2006 Transnistria held an "independence referendum." Although the Smirnov regime argued that the referendum demonstrated overwhelming support for independence, the vote was not monitored by any Western organizations, and no country has recognized the referendum or the independence of Transnistria.

Peacekeeping troops in Transnistria consist of 14,200 Russians equipped with 26 tanks and 90 armored vehicles, and peacekeepers, which include 498 Moldovans, 459 Russians, and about 500 Transnistrians. The OSCE periodically reviews the situation in Transnistria. It stresses that cooperation on all sides is necessary to reduce the arms that have been building up in Transnistria since the conflict began in 1991. Several participating states are willing to contribute either financially or with technical assistance to this plan.

ECONOMY

The Moldova Agroindbank (MAIB) is Moldova's largest commercial bank.

CHAPTER 4

MOLDOVA REMAINS THE POOREST country in Europe, despite recent progress in economic reform. It is landlocked, bounded by Ukraine in the north, the east, and the south and Romania in the west. In the past, economic activity was primarily agricultural, rural poverty was endemic, and the urban economy was based almost entirely on food processing and the production of consumer goods.

Although the breakaway Transnistria region covers only 12 percent of Moldova's territory, the region is of high economic importance for the country, as it straddles the major land routes to Russia and other strategically important export markets. In addition, most of Moldova's industry is located in Transnistria.

Poultry farmers proudly displaying their plump chickens.

MARKET ECONOMY

Moldova's economy resembles those of the Central Asian republics rather than those of countries on the western edge of the former Soviet Union. One limiting factor is that, except for very small gas and oil reserves, the country is totally dependent on energy imports, mainly from Russia. Industry accounts for less than 15 percent of its labor force, while agriculture's share is around 40.6 percent.

Like many of the other former Soviet republics, Moldova experienced a sharp downturn in its economy after the breakup of the Soviet Union in 1991. Since its economy was highly dependent on Russia for energy and raw materials, the breakdown in trade and energy shortages following the collapse of the Soviet Union had a serious effect, exacerbated at times by drought and civil conflict. Energy shortages also contributed to sharp production declines. After the Russian ruble devaluation of 1998, Moldova's economy underwent a prolonged recession.

Moldova has since made significant progress in economic reform, after it started to emerge from the recession in 2000. These reforms helped maintain Moldova's macroeconomic and financial stability under very difficult circumstances. It introduced its own currency, the leu, to replace the Russian ruble; liberalized prices for most of its commodities; backed land privatization; removed export controls; and freed interest rates. As a result, gross domestic product (GDP) growth was steady from 2000 to 2008, averaging between 3 percent and 7 percent.

Farmworkers shucking corn, another crop grown in Moldova.

AGRICULTURE

Moldova's proximity to the Black Sea gives it a mild and sunny climate, making it ideal for agriculture, which accounts for 40 percent of the country's GDP.

Crops such as berries, wine, tobacco, vegetables, sugar beets, potatoes, and sunflowers have traditionally accounted for the biggest share of agricultural production. The fertile soil also supports wheat, corn, barley, and soybeans. Its orchards produce significant amounts of fruit, including plums, peaches, apricots, and cherries.

Strips of terraced farmlands can be seen from an aerial view of Moldova. Working the land with modern machinery has increased production substantially.

Moldova also produces walnuts, sugar, vegetable oils, meat, and dairy products. Moldova's best-known wines come from its extensive and well-developed vineyards concentrated in the central and southern regions. In addition to world-class wine, Moldova produces liqueurs, brandies, and champagnes. Approximately half of Moldova's agricultural and food production is sold to former Soviet republics. Traditional markets are Russia, Ukraine, and Belarus.

In 2005 strained political relations led Russia to ban Moldovan agricultural products, and in 2006 Russia banned imports of Moldovan wines. This slowed down the economy greatly, compounded by a twofold increase in gas prices and a severe drought in 2007. The drought resulted in hundreds of millions of dollars in agricultural-sector losses and prompted widespread concerns about food availability. In response to a request for assistance, the United States delivered $350,000 worth of seeds to drought-ravaged farmers in time for fall planting.

Russia's wine ban was particularly painful for Moldova because, prior to the ban, Moldovan wines accounted for almost one-third of the country's

During the Soviet period, there was no private land, only state-owned collective farms. As part of the transition to a market economy, the government privatized most land, enterprises, houses, and apartments. By the end of 2000, nearly all of Moldova's agricultural land had been privatized from state to private ownership.

Privatization results in recent years were not so significant. With mass privatization over, the government has been selling state-owned residual shares in companies and focusing on efficient management of state assets. Total proceeds in 2007 amounted to $16.7 million. State-owned residual shares in 33 companies and one land plot in Chisinau were privatized in 2007. The government indefinitely postponed privatizations in the power, banking, telecommunications, and agribusiness sectors. In 2007 the parliament passed a law introducing new approaches to privatizing and managing state-owned assets.

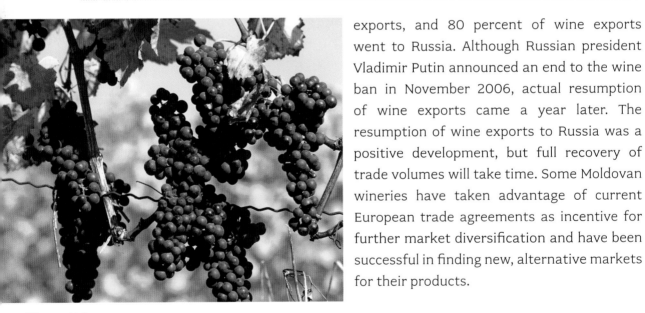

exports, and 80 percent of wine exports went to Russia. Although Russian president Vladimir Putin announced an end to the wine ban in November 2006, actual resumption of wine exports came a year later. The resumption of wine exports to Russia was a positive development, but full recovery of trade volumes will take time. Some Moldovan wineries have taken advantage of current European trade agreements as incentive for further market diversification and have been successful in finding new, alternative markets for their products.

Ripe and juicy Portugieser grapes growing at a vineyard in Moldova.

INDUSTRY

Food processing (including sugar and vegetable oils) is the largest domestic industry in Moldova, followed by energy production, engineering (agricultural machinery, foundry equipment, refrigerators, freezers, and washing machines) and metal processing, and other sectors, such as electronics, tobacco, hosiery, footwear, and textiles. In the processed fruit and vegetable sector, field tomatoes and apples account for 80 percent of all output. The remaining 20 percent of output includes canned goods, dehydrated fruits, purees for baby food, jams and preserves, and some specialty products.

Sugar beets are an important crop for Moldova. They are grown throughout the country and provide raw material for a substantial sugar-refining industry. About 16 million tons (16.3 million metric tons) of sugar beet are processed into 2 million tons (2.03 million metric tons) of white sugar each year. A persistent shortage of refined sugar in the region ensures a steady demand for sugar and sugar products, thus securing the future of Moldovan sugar producers.

Wine represents a major component of Moldova's economy, accounting for up to 50 percent of the total export income. The republic is known for its quality wines and is an important regional producer of grapes and grape products, with more than 150 wineries. Moldova's agricultural sector wasn't the only area of the economy hurt by Russia's 2006 ban on imports of wine. The main part of the recession hit the wine-producing industry, including production volumes. The biggest drop in the volume of wine production was in April 2006, when output shrunk by 75 percent. Total industrial manufacturing declined 6.7 percent over seven months of 2006, plunging the country's economy back into pre-2000 conditions.

The tobacco industry consists of eight fermentation plants and the Chisinau tobacco factory, which can produce 9.1 billion cigarettes a year. Tobacco processing continues to be one of Moldova's most important industries; during Soviet times, the republic produced 40 percent of the

A visitor examines Moldovan wines and brandy at a Wine Exhibition in Chisinau.

Moldova enjoys a favorable climate and good farmland but has no significant mineral deposits. As a result, the economy relies heavily on agriculture. It has to import energy sources such as petroleum, coal, and natural gas from Russia.

USSR's annual crop. Moldova has so far resisted pressure to privatize its tobacco industry.

More than 50 engineering plants produce electronic equipment, machinery, automation and telecommunications equipment, television sets, electric engines, pumps, tractors and other agricultural machinery, refrigerators, and other appliances. The light industry sector manufactures carpets, textiles, garments, and footwear. New industries such as scrap-metal processing, chemicals, and medical equipment have emerged since independence. In addition, the construction materials industry is expanding through exports of cement, gypsum, and ceramics, and through investment in civil engineering.

ENERGY

Among the most pressing concerns facing Moldova's economy is its lack of energy resources. The country has few oil reserves and no refineries. It depends almost entirely on Russia, Ukraine, and Romania for oil, coal, and natural gas, with only 3 percent of demand for primary energy covered by domestic sources. About 60 percent of energy consumption is in the form of electricity and heat, of which the industrial sector is the main consumer.

A high voltage line of electrotransfers, component parts of a power grid.

Small amounts of electric energy are being produced by the hydropower plants located on the Dniester and Prut rivers, but these are insufficient for the densely populated country. Other electricity-generating facilities, working on natural gas, produce only 25 to 30 percent of the total power the country consumes annually. Consumption of electricity in 2000 was 3.655 billion kilowatts.

In a bid to expand its energy resources and decrease its dependence on imports, Moldova is seeking alternative sources and is working to develop its renewable energy supplies, such as solar power, wind, and geothermal. Geothermal energy is harnessed using heat emitted from within the earth's crust, usually in the form of hot water or steam. The country also has a national energy-conservation program.

INFRASTRUCTURE

The infrastucture of Moldova is quite developed. Its road network is more than 10,439 miles (16,800 km) long, of which slightly more than 1,864 miles (3,000 km) are important highways, and the rest are local roads. Only 62 percent of the total road length has an improved asphalt pavement. Automobiles, buses, and trucks transport 96 percent of cargo and 85 percent of passengers.

As an agricultural country, Moldova depends on a reliable transportation network to ensure the efficient domestic movement of produce and the

In January 2006 Russian energy giant Gazprom temporarily cut off natural-gas supplies to Ukraine and Moldova and subsequently doubled the price of gas to Moldova. The price of Russian gas, which was $170 per 1,000 cubic m in 2007, is expected to reach average rates of $250 per 1,000 cubic m by 2011.

Trains transport most of the goods within, about, and outside Moldova.

A public bus in Chisinau.

export of agricultural goods. Railroads transport 95 percent of exports. The rail system extends for 803 miles (1,292 km) and carries a large amount of important exports and imports. In the freight sector, the split over the past six years has largely been about 72 percent for road and 28 percent for rail. Both road and rail freight traffic, however, have decreased as a result of the economic decline in Moldova during the past decade.

Air transportation is provided by private carriers and a state company. A project providing for the reconstruction and modernization of the Chisinau international air terminal is under way. Four airfields support international and domestic travel. The Dniester River is used for ferrying tourists and local cargo. The construction of a port and a fuel terminal is scheduled at the meeting point of the Prut and the Danube to serve tankers and other ships.

PUBLIC TRANSPORTATION

Moldova's well-developed public transportation network is largely credited to the extensive amount of highways, municipal, agricultural, and forestry roads.

Local transport in Moldova runs to trams, buses and the old-fashioned trolleybuses. However, traveling by road or rail are the two most common modes of transportation for local Moldovans.

Between states, too, Moldova is also well served by buses connecting Chisinau with Kiev, Bucharest, and key cities in Romania and Ukraine. A lot of these border crossings may take as long as 10 hours, but it provides a cheap means of transport for many rural dwellers who work in the cities.

Air transportation is crucial for developing countries and Moldova has made good progress restructuring civil aviation. Air transportation is represented by Air Moldova, as well as Moldavian Airlines and Air Moldova International, two commercial air carriers. Due to its central location between Eastern and Western Europe, the Chisinau airport is an excellent hub for international freight forwarders such as FedEx, UPS, and DHL.

Craftsmen building a new store in the village of Tataresi in southern Moldova.

MEASURING PROGRESS

During the transition years of 1991 to 1994, Moldova's GDP declined in most sectors—industry, agriculture, construction, and transportation. Inflation slowed in 1994 as a result of a tighter monetary policy.

Moldova's trade deficit can be attributed to a lack of energy resources and increases in energy prices, the lack of an external marketing network for Moldovan products, and the decline of production. Much depends on how successful the export of wine, canned fruits, and other agricultural products becomes.

Moldova in general and Chisinau (below) in particular have many traditional Balkan-style markets. There are mixed markets as well as specialized ones for all kinds of goods such as fresh produce. This "market economy" clearly outsells the regular shops. These markets are flourishing because of market liberalization and the economic downturn. Many educated professionals find it easier to earn money through such commercial activities than by practicing their professions.

The CIS takes 61 percent of Moldova's exports and provides 67 percent of its imports. After Russia, Ukraine, and Belarus, Uzbekistan is Moldova's fourth most important trade partner. The U.S. market remains unknown to Moldova, but opportunities are presenting themselves to local entrepreneurs.

The national currency, the Moldovan leu (plural: lei), was introduced in November 1993. The initial exchange rate was set at 3.85 lei to one U.S. dollar. The exchange rate of the Moldovan leu has demonstrated greater stability through the 1990s than those of the currencies of neighboring countries, including Russia, Romania, and Ukraine. To the Moldovans, this is encouraging.

ECONOMIC CHALLENGES

Moldova has faced many obstacles since independence. About 29.5 percent of the population lives below the poverty level. Living standards are poor for the great majority of Moldovans, particularly in rural areas. Total estimated unemployment is 1.5 percent. According to the World Bank, Moldova's per capita gross national income of $2,737.80 in 2008 made it the poorest country in Europe. In 2008, the average monthly wage was $228.15.

Roughly 20 percent of Moldova's economically active population work abroad. The Moldovan economy continues to depend greatly on remittances sent from Moldovans working abroad. Figures from the World Bank show that remittances amounted to 38.3 percent of the country's GDP in 2008. These inflows have increased to around $1.5 billion a year.

Moldova has had mixed success in economic reform. The republic has privatized its small- and midsize-business sector and has had success in privatizing agricultural land. It has succeeded in achieving a measure of macroeconomic stability, including the stabilization of Moldova's national currency, the leu. Moldova's small economy is highly vulnerable to external shocks, however. Following the economic difficulties caused by the Russian currency crisis of 1998, inflation rose as high as 13.1 percent in 2007. The National Bank of Moldova had the difficult task of containing the stubbornly high inflation.

The global financial crisis also had a negative impact on Moldova. The leu weakened and remains under pressure. Remittances dropped as Moldovans lost jobs in other countries. Moldova's GDP dropped by 6.9 percent in the first quarter of 2009 and is expected to fall further.

A penniless Moldovan woman begging for money. Many Moldovans were affected by the economic downturn that accompanied the breakup of Moldova from the Soviet Union.

ENVIRONMENT

The river rapids and waterfalls in Moldova
are a breathtaking sight to behold.

CHAPTER 5

MOLDOVA IS A RELATIVELY flat country, with one-third of its land covered by fertile plains and terraces. Colorful orchards, fields of grain, and sunflowers dot the countryside. Being mostly flat and well drained, Moldova has no topographical constraints to growth.

It is a country blessed with rich soils and a high percentage of arable land. Its terrain is further endowed with minerals and sedimentary rocks, including sand, clay, gravel, gypsum, and limestone.

Vibrantly beautiful sunflowers fill Moldova's countryside.

Unfortunately, economic development and agricultural pollution have led to a massive reduction in Moldova's biodiversity, particularly its steppe and wetland habitats. Heavy use of agricultural chemicals, including banned pesticides such as DDT (dichlorodiphenyltrichloroethane, a colorless, odorless water-insoluble insecticide), along with poor farming methods and overexploitation have resulted in soil degradation and contaminated groundwater. Soil erosion washes away an estimated 26 million tons (26.4 million metric tons) of fertile soil annually. It also leads to landslides, which are a natural hazard in Moldova.

Air, water, and industrial pollution are widespread and are the attributed cause of Moldova's high rates of abnormal births and infant mortalities. In many parts of the country, levels of nitrate, chloride, iron, and fecal bacteria are well above the levels considered safe by the World Health Organization (WHO).

LAND

The soils of Moldova are varied and highly fertile, with chernozem—rich black soils—covering 75 percent of the republic. Moldova's agricultural productivity is due largely to its rich soils. The best chernozem, which feeds the growth of grain, tobacco, and sugar beets, is found in the north and low-lying parts of the central and Dniester uplands, as well as in the left-bank regions. Excessive use of chemical fertilizers, pesticides, and herbicides during the Soviet period, however, resulted in extensive contamination of Moldova's soil and groundwater.

For more than 50 years, Moldova was part of the former Soviet Union, with an economy based on agriculture and food processing. During this time, 75 percent of the land was devoted to agriculture. Small farms were converted into large agricultural enterprises and state farms, and they were saturated with chemicals to increase production.

Unsustainable use of land and heavy machinery resulted in severe degradation of the environment. Large cattle, pig, and poultry farms that lacked proper waste management facilities were established near major rivers. The discharge of untreated animal waste and manure was until recently a major pollutant of Moldova's groundwater and drinking water supply.

FORESTS

Forests in Moldova cover about 13 percent of the country's territory, or 951,356 acres (385,000 ha). Northern and central Moldova is a forest zone, while a steppe belt encompasses the south. Moldova's steppes were originally grass covered, but now most of them are cultivated. The most common trees are hornbeam and oak, followed by linden, maple, wild pear, and wild cherry. Beech forests are commonly found around the Ikel and Bac rivers.

Moldova's forest biodiversity is rich—its forests contain more than 1,800 vascular plant species, 46 of which are endangered or vulnerable, and 1,000 mushroom species. Terrestrial vertebrates number about 172, while insect species number close to 10,000.

The republic has five scientific reserves, two of which are forest reserves, while three are forest-aquatic reserves. Totaling an area of 47,884 acres (19,378 ha), the reserves protect natural areas of bird migration, old beech and oak forests, and major waterways. Moldova's oldest and most popular reserve is the Codri Reserve. It is home to some 924 plant species, 138 bird species, and 45 species of mammals.

Forests such as these are in danger of disappearing as Moldovan industries flourish and require more of the already scarce land.

Poor forest management, however, has led to a reduction in forest quality and a decrease of biodiversity in certain areas. Very little research and training is carried out in the areas of biodiversity protection and conservation, the development and management of natural areas, and the protection of vulnerable and endangered species of animals and plants. Like many other former Soviet republics, Moldova lacks the financial resources and institutional capacity to implement the provisions of the Convention on Biological Diversity, to which Moldova is a signatory.

Other threats to forest biodiversity are deforestation, unauthorized grazing, and pollution due to municipal waste and unregulated tourism. Extensive deforestation has resulted in soil erosion, wind damage, a drop in the groundwater table, flooding, and loss of fauna. Well aware of the propensity of problems caused by such a great loss of woodlands, environmentalists and scientists have lobbied for increased afforestation plans. As a result, large-scale reforestation projects have been carried on since the early 1990s. The projects, however, have met with resistance from farmers who have been concerned that their agricultural and grazing lands would be converted into less profitable forests.

A boy passes through a landscape of trash generated by locals.

NATIONAL PARKS

Moldova's sole national park, the Lower Dniester National Park (Parcul National Nistrul Inferior), is run by Biotica, a nonprofit environmental organization. The park covers more than 148,263 acres (60,000 ha) of land southeast of Chisinau, hugging the Dniester River southward to the border of Ukraine. It includes wetlands, forests, lakes, and farmland, as well as some 40 archaeological sites, observation points, villages, and some of Moldova's best vineyards.

These can be accessed via excursions and rural homestays organized by Biotica. There are also two natural areas protected by the state: Padurea Domneasca and Prutul de Jos. There are plans to establish a second national park, Codrii Orheiului.

WATER SUPPLY

Moldova has a well-developed network of rivers and streams, all draining south to the Black Sea. The marshy lower reaches of Moldova's rivers provide respite for wild geese, migratory ducks, and herons, whereas white-tailed sea eagles are found in the floodplain forests. Underground water, extensively used for the republic's water supply, includes some 2,200 natural springs.

The lakes in Moldova are home to many species of wildlife.

Moldova receives 3,592 gallons (13,597 l) of water annually, with the Dniester River supplying 56 percent of the country's needs and the Prut River providing 16 percent. But in spite of the country's 3,621 water courses, occasional water shortages occur due to low precipitation and high evaporation rates. These shortages lead to crop failure, and rivers and wells drying up. To add to the problem, the Prut and Dniester are contaminated by intensive agricultural production and industrial wastes.

Although Moldova has more than 3,000 rivers and streams, only about one-tenth of them exceed 6.2 miles (10 km) in length, and even fewer exceed 62 miles (100 km). Many of the small, shallow streams dry up during the summer. Moldova does not have any large lakes, and all of its larger rivers originate outside its borders.

Since water resources are of particular importance to Moldova, water pollution is viewed as a significant threat. The republic has difficulties securing adequate supplies of potable water and reducing the pollution levels in existing supplies. Only 8 percent of Moldova's water comes from aquifers, and only 50 percent of this meets drinking standards.

WATER SERVICES

Moldova's municipal water sector is still suffering from years of neglect and underinvestment. Raw water resources are polluted, and water treatment plants are no longer able to meet quality standards. Many of the smaller towns get their water supply from groundwater sources that do not meet hygiene standards. These towns typically experience daily power cuts, resulting in a lack of water pressure in the network and a reduction in water quality.

As for wastewater treatment, most such plants in Moldova were designed for both mechanical and biological treatment. However, as a result of inadequate maintenance, regular power cuts, low water pressure in the network, and limited finances, most wastewater treatment plants operate on mechanical treatment only.

Moldova's National Environmental Action Plan (NEAP) has calculated that polluted drinking water leads to 950 to 1,850 premature deaths annually, and 2 to 4 million days of illness annually. The cost to the economy is estimated to be 5 to 10 percent of the GDP.

STATE ACCOUNTABILITY

The Republic of Moldova has two tiers of local government: municipal (villages and towns) and *judets* (zhu-DETS), or counties. The responsibility of regulating environmental standards lies with the environmental inspectors at the *judets* level. The provision of services, such as municipal solid waste management, water supply, and wastewater collection and treatment, is the responsibility of the municipalities.

Many of Moldova's local officials, however, have very limited knowledge of the country's environmental issues. They are faced with an astonishing range of environmental and social problems at a time when there is strong pressure for change. They must also come to terms with tougher environmental laws influenced by the EU, such as Moldova's Framework Directive on Water.

What's more, Moldova's environmental issues are becoming more and more acute and expensive to solve. In 2007 Moldova suffered a severe drought, which dried up its water resources and forced farmers to abandon their crops and sell their livestock. In November 2000, a severe ice storm caused massive disruption and chaos. Temperatures hovered around -77°F (-61°C) for long periods of time, destroying thousands of crops, orchards, and forests, with the weight of the ice bringing down trees and power lines. Budget constraints made it impossible for local administrators to respond effectively to these and other challenges.

With the increasing number of manufacturing and refinery plants, the quality of air in Moldova is on the decline.

With funding from the Environ Foundation and in collaboration with Romanian nongovernmental organization (NGO) Prietenii Pamantului (Earth Friends) and British NGO Powerful Information, Craion (an abbreviation for "Information and Supporting Regional Center for NGOs") Contact Cahul will work with mayors and local councillors as well as environmental and community development NGOs in Moldova's South Development Region to help them manage their natural resources in a sustainable and acceptable way and to help improve amenities for local residents. It will train 24 officials and representatives from 15 communities in the Cahul region in environmental issues and techniques of public education as well as organize meetings to inform residents about the threats posed by certain practices and climate change and the implications of Moldova's environmental legislation on resource use and pollution.

Through workshops on groundwater pollution, sewage and wastewater treatment, solid waste disposal, and local biodiversity, the organization hopes to improve environmental decision making at the local level and to generate more interest in environmental issues. It also aims to get residents more involved in decisions that affect their community and improve cooperation among local communities, environmental institutions, local government, and NGOs.

KEEPING FARMS IN CHECK

Since Moldova's independence from the Soviet Union, the country's agricultural sector has undergone significant structural changes. Former large-scale enterprises and farms have been reorganized into smaller private farms and farming associations, as they were in the old days. The large livestock farms have been dismantled, and the majority of livestock are now kept in small and midsize farms.

However, according to the APCP, today's farmers and landowners lack the farming experience, technical skills, and financial resources for sustainable farm management. It has been estimated that more than 988,422 acres (400,000 ha) of private livestock farms are moderately or highly degraded. Nutrient runoff to the rivers stems from unsustainable crop- and soil-management practices; overexploitation and illegal cutting of trees; inappropriate storage and disposal of animal manure and waste; overgrazing; and mismanagement of wetlands.

The continued lack of effective manure-management practices is leading to increased groundwater pollution and is damaging the drinking water supply of rural communities in Moldova. According to the APCP, samples analyzed from about 70 percent of rural wells, which are the main source of drinking water for rural communities, revealed high nitrogen levels in excess of the maximum acceptable levels.

MOLDOVANS

A young Moldovan girl proudly holds up a bunch of ripe grapes.

CHAPTER 6

MOLDOVA HAS A POPULATION density of 336 persons per square mile (131 persons per square km). Most of its population lives in the northern and central parts of the country. During the Soviet period, Moldova had the highest population density among the Soviet republics.

Until 2002, Moldova ranked 116 out of 412 countries as one of the most densely populated European countries in the world. In comparison, the United States has a density of only 60 people per square mile (23 per square km).

Although a melting pot of different cultures, the multiethnic Moldovans live harmoniously with one another.

One of the residential districts in Chisinau.

POPULATION TRENDS

The multiethnic population of Moldova reflects the complexity of its history. Of its 4.7 million people, excluding the breakaway region of Transnistria, 76 percent are Moldovan, 8 percent Ukrainian, 6 percent Russian, 4 percent Gagauz, 2 percent Roma, 2 percent Bulgarian, and 2 percent others. Smaller ethnic minorities such as the Gagauz (Turkish Christians) and Bulgarians reside in rural towns in the south. These rural Gagauz and Bulgarian communities have their own degree of regional autonomy. Unemployment is relatively low at 2.6 percent in 2009, while 65 percent of Moldovans are in the workforce. As of January 1, 2009, ,about 29.5 percent of the population were reported to be living below the poverty line.

WHERE PEOPLE LIVE

Moldovans reside in 65 cities and towns and more than 1,575 villages. Only 53 percent of Moldovans live in cities. More than 60 percent of the urban population is concentrated in Chisinau, Balti, Tiraspol, and Tighina, with more than 33 percent in the capital of Chisinau. Almost 68 percent of the rural population resides in towns and villages while the others continue living on their family property in the country. While it is not uncommon for urban Moldovans to adopt a Russian linguistic and national identity, Moldova's rural populations, who traditionally have had less access to education and power, tend to maintain their ethnic identities and language.

About 76 percent of the population are native Moldovans, while the other 24 percent are primarily Ukrainians, Russians, and Gagauz. There are also a small number of Bulgarians, Roma, and Jews, as well as Belarusians, Poles, and Germans. Most Moldovans make no distinction between the Romanian and Moldovan languages.

THE ISSUE OF ETHNICITY

Moldova joins two regions, Bessarabia and Transnistria, into one country. Bessarabia consists predominantly of ethnic Romanians and constitutes the western half of the country. Transnistria is Slavic, and its people are ethnic Ukrainians and Russians. Viewed as a whole, Moldova has a majority population of ethnic Romanians. Despite Soviet efforts to subjugate them to slavery, most ethnic Romanians maintained their identity and looked to Romania as the source of their culture. When the Soviet Union crumbled, Moldova asserted its independence, although people were far from unanimous on the issue. The nationalists eventually succeeded. Moldova sought to distance itself from Russia. But the Transnistrians wanted no part of independent Moldova, its ethnic-Romanian nationalists, or reunification with Romania, where they would be a small minority instead of a powerful political force.

Ethnic Russian and Romanian children enjoying a swim at a pool.

While the language and culture of the majority is largely Romanian, the Soviet period saw a dominance of Russian language in economics, politics, education, and any attempts at modernization. In addition, Russian influence saw a large influx of Ukrainians and Russians migrating to Moldova, particularly to its urban centers. Stalin further strengthened his hold by making Russian the official language and favoring ethnic Russians for government positions. He was able to exert power over Moldovans by reducing their population majority, concentrating the industrial centers in Russian-speaking Ukrainian-dominated areas, and increasing their dependence on such areas for industrial produce. As a result, Moldovan urbanites in general, despite their ethnic backgrounds, have adopted the Russian language and national identity to some degree. The rural-urban divide was also obvious, with Russian spoken widely in cities and national languages spoken in rural areas.

People walk on a street in the center of Bender, a city located in the breakaway region of Transnistria.

Complicating this struggle of identities have been regional conflicts involving minority groups such as ethnic Russians and Gagauz fighting for more autonomy and independence. The military conflict between Transnistria and Moldova in 1992 is an example of this. Transnistria and Moldova went to war when the Soviet empire was dissolved and Transnistria tried to claim independence from Moldova. The dispute was said to be driven by culture, religion, and ethnic nationalism. The region successfully defeated Moldovan forces, with the help of Russia. Today the Russian-speaking population of Transnistria continues to maintain an independent Soviet quality, although the territory is unrecognized as independent. While a cease-fire has been maintained ever since, the Council of Europe recognizes Transnistria as a "frozen conflict" region.

MOLDOVAN CHARACTER

Moldovans have managed to maintain strong family ties, tradition, a rich culture, and a love of beauty and the arts. Under Soviet rule, everything was done for the good of the community. This spirit is slowly dying out. In its

A typical Moldovan family.

The problem of ethnicity has dominated the political scene in Moldova since the late 1980s, leading to armed conflicts in 1992 by groups of ethnic Russians and Gagauz in the east and the south demanding autonomy and special political status.

Moldovan women coming together to chat. Rural folks enjoy forging close ties with their neighbors.

place is the freedom to act according to one's interests. But this does not mean they have become self-centered. Moldovans are extremely friendly and kind. This is especially so in the villages, where the communal bond is close-knit. Moldovans love to socialize and make people feel comfortable. Friends will stop by each other's homes without prior notice because they know they will be welcome. People are also not aggressive or competitive by nature. Moldovans generally do not enter into fighting with their own people. Any hostility or violence toward others is usually caused by the potent force of nationalism, where people hold different political opinions.

LOCAL CUSTOMS

Moldovan men greet each other with a handshake. When a man sees a male acquaintance in a group and greets him with a handshake, it would be impolite not to shake the hands of all the other males in the group as well. Moldovan women do not shake hands, however. In either a business or a social setting, a nod of the head is acceptable when greeting a woman.

In Moldova, shoes that are worn outdoors are removed when entering a home or an apartment. Moldovans normally change into slippers indoors. A host would be extremely offended if guests were to wear their shoes in his home.

TRADITIONAL DRESS

A distinctive feature of the Moldovan national dress is the embroidery on both men's and women's clothes. The rich colors of red, black, and gold embroidery complement each other and contrast with a white background. A woman's blouse is loose-fitting with three-quarter or full-length sleeves, worn with a white skirt. Over the skirt, a dark-colored apron with woven geometric patterns is tied at the waist with a sash. Regional differences are reflected in the colors and patterns of embroidery used. Cotton and silk, or wool for the winter, are the preferred fabrics. These clothes are traditionally spun and sewn by women. Women wear colored scarves with a white border of lace on their heads and tied under at the nape. Strings of beads around the neck and long dangling pearl earrings complete the outfit.

The men's national dress is a long-sleeve white shirt, worn with narrow trousers that are secured at the waist with a sash or a leather belt. An embroidered sleeveless vest is worn over the shirt. Headgear for men is a tall hat made of lambskin, felt, or even straw for the summer. Traditional footwear for both sexes is the moccasin, a type of soft leather slipper.

Boys and girls in their traditional outfits.

LIFESTYLE

A mother takes a relaxing stroll with her children.

CHAPTER 7

INCE 1991, LIFE FOR MOLDOVANS has changed, whether they live in urban centers or rural areas. Communist control, collective farms, and social protection have been replaced by the market economy. Such adjustments can be very difficult for people who have depended on the Communist system all their lives.

Moldovan women working on a communal farm.

Corruption and crime have increased significantly, and living standards have been reduced. Now there is a growing gap between the rich and the poor. Despite these difficulties, Moldovans have retained their core values and traditions. Family, friends, and village communities remain close-knit.

In general, Moldovan life revolves around their love of family, care for the land, development as a nation, and ties with the larger European society. Chisinau, the republic's capital, offers modern European city living, whereas the countryside offers rustic charm from the past. Most Moldovans hope that in the 21st century, with the worst behind them, they can enjoy the fruits of capitalism that they have been promised.

FAMILY AND KINSHIP

It is not unusual to find three generations of a family living in the same house in Moldova. Although this can mainly be attributed to the difficulty of finding housing, it is also a reflection of Moldovan family values. The family is very important to Moldovans, and the average urban family has two or three children. Rural families may have more children. Children generally grow up close to their grandparents, who teach them songs and fairy tales. Girls are expected to help their mothers from an early age and to take care of younger siblings.

Grandparents taking care of their grandson. Moldovans are often very close to their families.

From the time they are young children, Moldovans are taught to respect and care for older people. Thus there are few nursing homes for the elderly and the disabled. Within a family, if there are older members, the rest would try their best to provide for them. Placing a family member in an aged-care institution is definitely a last resort. Relatives support one other in performing agricultural and other tasks as well as in ceremonial obligations. The godparenthood system regulates mutual obligations between the parties. Godparents are responsible for the children they sponsor at baptism, especially marriage and the building of a house. Godparenthood is inherited through the generations; however, it is also common for this role to be negotiated independently of previous ties.

Families and friends getting together for a meal. Despite busy lifestyles, Moldovans often find the time to catch up with one another.

SOCIAL CUSTOMS

Moldovans greatly enjoy visiting friends and relatives. Most socializing takes place in the home. On special occasions, guests are treated to feasts. Otherwise, people sit in the kitchen or the living room and chat for hours. Hosts generally provide guests with coffee, tea, wine, or cognac. Vodka is popular among the Russian minority. Guests often bring small gifts, and hosts, especially in rural areas, usually reciprocate with a small gift such as a cake "for the next morning" or wine. It is proper to drink at least a symbolic amount of wine during a meal or in a ritual context to honor the host and toast the health of the people present. Occasionally in villages, toasting with the left hand may not be regarded as proper.

A host pours wine for his guest. The hospitable Moldovans enjoy inviting friends over often.

Food is almost always prepared by the women in the family; it is considered embarrassing for a man to admit he cooks. When guests are present, the hosts offer additional helpings; it is polite to decline two or three times before accepting. Leaving food on the plate may be considered a sign that a guest has not enjoyed the meal. It is also improper to blow one's nose at the table. Smoking in homes is an uncommon practice; both hosts and guests usually go outside or onto the balcony to smoke. In villages, it is highly improper for women to smoke in public.

Interaction differs in urban and rural areas. In the villages, people are friendly and greet passersby without prior acquaintance; in the cities, there is a greater anonymity, although people interact with strangers in certain situations—for example, on public transportation. Foreign visitors are considered honored guests and are treated with great respect and hospitality. Moldovans are usually very keen to hear what foreigners think of their country. Visitors, in turn, are struck by the warmth of the Moldovan people.

FOOD CUSTOMS

Orthodox Christian baptisms, funerals, and weddings are accompanied by large gatherings where several meat and vegetable dishes, desserts, and cakes as well as wine are served. Homemade vodka and brandy are also offered. At Easter, a special bread, *pasca* (pas-KUH), is baked in every household, and eggs are painted in various colors. Families go to the cemetery to commemorate their dead kin; they eat food at the graves, drink wine, and share their meals with each other as they remember the dead.

LIFE EVENTS

To Moldovans, baptisms, weddings, and funerals are the most important life-cycle rituals and are combined with church attendance and social gatherings. Orthodox Christians typically marry in a church ceremony, which is followed

A happy bride and groom with their wedding entourage.

by a party with dancing and plenty to eat and drink. In the rural areas, any stranger who enters the village on the day of the marriage is invited to join in the festivities and is welcomed as part of the family. Local musicians play lively music, and tables are set up in a central communal area for the feast. Giving money rather than presents is a traditional custom, and a plate is passed around to collect money for the couple.

Newlyweds usually live together with the groom's parents until they can build a house in the village or rent an apartment in town. In the villages, there is a general rule of ultimogeniture: The youngest son and his family live with the parents, and he inherits the contents of the household.

Another happy occasion Moldovans celebrate is the birth of a child. If the infant's parents are Orthodox Christians, the child is christened in the church, and guests are invited to the parents' house for refreshments. Babies are taken care of by their mothers and grandmothers. In villages, babies are wrapped in blankets during the very early months, and cloth diapers are used.

Funerals are solemn events, and the deceased are treated with utmost respect. Ideally the body is laid in an open casket and watched over for three days. Relatives and friends come to the house to pay their respects to the family. Food and drink, prepared by the family, are served to the mourners. A mixture of cooked wheat and sugar called *colivă* (Kol-ly-va) is prepared

Family members visiting the grave of their loved one.

and offered to guests. Usually the burial is within three days of death. For Jews, the ceremony takes place within two days. Both Christians and Jews regularly visit the gravesites of their loved ones.

RECREATION

In their spare time, Moldovans visit friends, go to the movies, or read. Football, badminton, basketball, volleyball, swimming, and ice-skating are popular sports among teenagers and young adults. Public facilities are available, but most are in need of repair. Many Moldovans love music and the arts, and they particularly enjoy attending concerts and festivals. Folk music is especially popular at national festivals.

No doubt because of the number of young people who flock to the capital for work and study, Chisinau has a thriving nightlife, boasting a multitude of clubs with cutting-edge decor and design. Outside of the capital, however, nightlife is very limited, with most towns having one drinking spot and being very provincial in outlook and facilities.

RITUALS

The Orthodox calendar dictates rituals and celebrations throughout the year, such as Christmas, Easter, and several saints' days. Some of the customary rules include fasting or avoiding meat and meat fat as well as restrictions on washing, bathing, and working at particular times. Easter is celebrated in church and by visiting the graves of kin. Candles are an inseparable part of rituals for Moldovans; people buy candles when they enter the church and light them in front of the icons or during rituals.

ARCHITECTURE

During the Soviet period, there was no private land, only state-owned collective farms. Since 1990, as part of the transition to a market economy, the privatization of land as well as houses and apartments has taken place. However, the process is still under way and has faced fierce resistance from agro-industrial complexes.

Chisinau's city center was constructed in the 19th century by the Russians. Official buildings and those erected by the early bourgeoisie are in a neoclassical style of architecture; there are also many small one-story houses in the center, and the outskirts are dominated by typical Soviet-style residential buildings. Small towns (mainly enlarged villages) also have examples of Soviet-style administration buildings and apartment blocks. Depending on their original inhabitants, villages have typical Moldovan, Ukrainian, Gagauz, Bulgarian, or German houses and a Soviet-style infrastructure (cultural center, school, local council buildings). Houses have their own gardens and usually their own vineyards and are surrounded by low metal-ornamented bars.

The beautiful national history museum in Chisinau.

Newly built ornamented houses and villas, cars (especially Western cars with tinted windows), cellular telephones, and fashionable clothes are the most distinguishing symbols of wealth in Moldova. Consumer goods brought from abroad (Turkey, Romania, Germany) function as status symbols in cities and rural areas.

EDUCATION

Moldova has an adult literacy rate of 99 percent. Education is higher among the female population than the male population and is compulsory for children ages 7 to 16. They attend 10 years of basic education followed by either technical school or higher education.

Under the Soviet system, education was free for all. Most schools were taught in the Russian language. Moldovans who were educated in Russian-speaking schools still have difficulty expressing themselves in Moldovan in instances other than daily encounters. Moldovans who were born after 1980 tend to speak less and less Russian, a trend that could lead to growing problems of interethnic communication.

A few universities still continue from the Soviet period, together with about 50 technical and vocational schools. The State University of Moldova, the Technical University of Moldova, the State Agricultural University of Moldova, and the Academy of Music, Theater, and Fine Arts are some of the major higher education institutions, all of which are in Chisinau. As a result of economic difficulties, Moldovans sometimes complete higher education in their late 30s, after establishing a family.

A moderate amount of Moldovans go on to pursue higher education, with 114,900 students in its universities. The country also has 38 institutions of higher education, of which 25 are private and 13 state-supported.

SOCIAL STRATIFICATION

Social stratification in Moldova is determined mainly by economic and political power. Large landowners, or boyars, disappeared after the establishment of Soviet power and the formation of state-owned collective farms. There is an emerging class of high-ranking officials and managers who had access to state enterprises or funds in the Soviet period and appropriated some of those resources during the transitional phase, as well as young entrepreneurs who amassed wealth after the introduction of a market economy through new business ventures.

After the demise of the Soviet Union, those who had higher positions in government tended to be Moldovans, while Russians dominated the private sector. Urban workers have maintained their rural connections and grow fruit and vegetables on small plots of land in the towns.

GENDER ROLES

Women in both the urban and rural areas carry the burden of domestic duties and childcare in addition to working outside the home. As a result of tradition and economic necessity, women often engage in domestic food-processing activities in the summer to provide home-canned food for the bleak winter months.

Although men seem to have more decision-making power in the public and private spheres, women generally act as the organizers of daily and ritual life. They organize social gatherings, gift-giving practices, and the infrastructure of numerous official and semiofficial events. There are no moral restrictions on women's participation in public life, although many women refrain from taking up executive positions and tend to give priority to family and domestic life.

A woman working in her office in Chisinau. More women are joining the workforce in an attempt to become financially independent.

RELIGION

The interior of a beautifully
adorned cathedral in Chisinau.

A

LMOST 98 PERCENT OF MOLDOVANS, including the overwhelming majority of ethnic Moldovans, Russians, Gagauz, and Ukrainians, are Eastern Orthodox Christians.

They belong primarily to one of two denominations: the Moldovan Orthodox Church (under the Russian Orthodox Church) and the Bessarabian Orthodox Church (under the Romanian Orthodox Church). About 3.6 percent of the population belongs to the Old Rite Russian Orthodox Church (Old Believers).

A view of the Saint Nicholas Church (*Sfantul Ierarh Nicolae*) from the Condrita Monastery in Moldova.

A roadside shrine commemorates Christ's crucifixion.

The other religious denominations are Roman Catholic, Uniate, Jewish, Armenian Apostolic, Seventh-day Adventist, Baptist, Pentecostal, Jehovah's Witness, Lutheran, Presbyterian, and Mormon. There are more than 1,030 churches, and 36 monasteries. The Jewish community has about 31,300 members. Its numbers had been greatly reduced by wars, the Holocaust, and emigration to Israel. There are also communities of Muslims and Baha'is. About one-fifth of Moldovans consider themselves nonreligious.

During the Soviet period, the Communist government strictly limited the activities and practices of all religions. Since the collapse of the Soviet Union, however, most religions have undergone a revival and have worked toward regaining their former prominence. Citizens in independent Moldova today have much greater religious freedom than they did under the Soviet regime.

EASTERN ORTHODOX CHURCH

The Eastern Orthodox Church is a Christian branch that separated from the Roman Catholic Church in the 11th century. The split between the two churches was related to the division of the Roman Empire into Eastern and Western halves, the Eastern center being the city of Constantinople (now known as Istanbul) and the Western center being Rome. Conflict over issues of doctrine led to an irreconcilable division, and the Patriarch of Constantinople and the Pope of Rome excommunicated each other. Following this divorce, the two branches went in quite distinct directions, largely due to the different cultures of the west and the east.

For Eastern Christianity, mysticism is extremely important, and the idea of grace and the redeeming power of God's love is paramount. Eastern Christianity is widely practiced in Greece, Eastern Europe, the Middle East,

The Parcul Catedralei Orthodox church in Chisinau.

and North Africa. According to many authorities, one of the reasons the Eastern liturgy has made a stronger impact on the Christian Church than its Western counterpart is that it has always been viewed as a total experience, appealing simultaneously to the emotional, intellectual, and aesthetic aspects of humanity. Western Christianity, on the other hand, portrays God as ultimately a judge. Followers of Western Christianity believe that one's actions in life will influence whether one can go to heaven after death.

Since 1992 the Bessarabian Orthodox Church has been negotiating with the Chisinau government to grant it legal status, but each of its formal appeals was refused until 2002, when the government finally registered the church. Despite fierce opposition from the rival Moldovan Orthodox Church, the government finally bowed to pressure from the European Court of Human Rights (ECHR) and the Council of Europe Parliamentary Assembly, which had given the Moldovan government a deadline of July 31, 2002, to register the church. The ECHR fined the government €27,025 ($24,400) for its refusal to register the church. The compensation was paid to the church for pecuniary and nonpecuniary damage and legal expenses.

RELIGION UNDER SOVIET RULE

The Soviet government strictly limited religious activity and ordered the destruction of Orthodox churches in an attempt to destroy religion. Clergies were punished and sometimes imprisoned for leading services, but most Orthodox believers continued to practice their religion in secret. By the beginning of World War II, the church structure was almost completely destroyed throughout the country. Many priests were driven away.

The catastrophic course of combat in the beginning of World War II forced Stalin to mobilize all national resources for defense, including the Orthodox Church as the people's moral force. Without delay, churches were opened for services, and clerics were released from prisons. Even after the war, the church hierarchy was greatly expanded, although some members of the clergy were still occasionally arrested. This process can be described as a rapprochement between church and state. The church, however, remained under state control. A new and widespread persecution of the church was subsequently instituted under the leadership of Nikita Khrushchev and Leonid Brezhnev. Then, beginning in the late 1980s under Mikhail Gorbachev, new political and social freedoms resulted in the lifting of the remaining restrictions. The collapse of the Soviet Union in 1991 led to complete religious freedom. Since then, churches have been restored and repaired in towns and villages. There is, however, a chronic lack of priests, and the recruitment of seminarians, or students training to be priests, is very low.

Three priests preside over a festive occasion.

ORTHODOX VIEW

The concept that the church is most authentic when the faithful are gathered together in worship is a basic expression of the Eastern Orthodox experience.

This explains the fundamental structure of the Orthodox Church, with the bishop functioning as a teacher and high priest in the liturgy. A richness of faith, spiritual significance, and variety of worship represents one of the most significant factors in this church's continuity and identity. It helps to account for the survival of Christianity during the many centuries of Muslim rule in the Middle East and the Balkans, when the liturgy was the only source of religious knowledge or experience. The Orthodox Church has a firm conviction that the liturgy is the main vehicle and experience of true Christian beliefs. Consequently, reform of the liturgy is often considered equivalent to a reform of the faith itself. However inconvenient this conservatism may be, the Orthodox liturgy has preserved many essential Christian values transmitted directly from the experience of the early church.

Religion is an important part of the lives of Moldovans, including soldiers.

The splendid Teodor Tiron monastery (*Catedrala Sfîntul Mare Mucenic Teodor Tiron*), an Orthodox church in Chisinau.

CHURCH ARCHITECTURE

The highly decorated style of the Eastern Orthodox Church originated in the Byzantine era. This style of architecture and icon painting has since grown into an important Moldovan art. The physical splendor of the churches is emphasized, and a standard style—the cross inscribed in a rectangle and the dome supported on piers—became the accepted style for Orthodox churches. Over time, windows were narrowed, roofs became steeper, and flat-dome profiles assumed the rotund form, which eventually became the most notable feature of Orthodox church architecture.

After Constantinople fell to the Turks in 1453, Russia launched a large-scale church building program. Church architecture began to lose the special features associated with the Byzantine heritage, becoming more national in character and increasingly illustrating the taste and thought of the people. The most important change in Russian church design in the 16th century was the introduction of the tiered tower and the tent-shaped roof, first developed in wood by Russia's carpenters. The basic types and structural forms of the Russian multicolumned and tented churches were fully developed in the 16th century.

IMPORTANCE OF ICONS

Icon *is a Greek word meaning "image." Icons are usually painted on a wooden base known as an icon board. The board consists of several parts bound together at the back by planks. The icon is placed on the face side of the board in a shallow rectangle or square groove (ark). Before painting begins, the board is covered with fabric, primed with a mixture of natural glue and chalk, and then coated with an initial layer of dark reddish brown or greenish paint. Where needed, the color is made lighter with ochre or whiting. Radial lines of gold are painted on the top of regular paint.*

Icon painting flourishes in monasteries. According to custom, an icon artist is expected to be a person of high morals and Christian ideals who prepares for his work by fasting and praying. The iconography is not a creation of the artist's imagination or whim but follows a pattern and subject prescribed by church tradition. Sometimes icons had metal covers, called oklads, *made to protect them from human handling in devotions, to enhance their beauty, or as memorials. The* oklads *often were made of silver or gilded silver, and the metal was cut out to reveal the painted faces, hands, and feet of the icon beneath. Some* oklads *were studded with precious gemstones, diamonds, and pearls.*

In a church, small icons are set on portable, cloth-draped lecterns, and large ones are hung on the walls. Beeswax candles are burned nearby, the icons are kissed and touched, and incense is lit in front of them as acts of devotion. Icons are blessed with holy water and carried in processions both inside and outside the church. An icon of one of the 12 special liturgical feast days is often displayed on a lectern in the center of the church on the day of the feast. An icon of a special saint whose memory the church is honoring or an icon of the church's patron saint may also be placed in this central location. The faithful pray, make the sign of the cross, and display profound reverences, such as bowing, kneeling, kissing, and touching the forehead to the icon. Icons are venerated but never worshiped.

These acts of respect, handed down from ancient cultural traditions, still survive worldwide in the Orthodox Church. In Orthodox homes, icons are displayed in special places of honor. To the Orthodox Christian, an icon is a constant reminder of God's presence in his church, his home, and in his life.

THE ROLE OF HYMNS

Throughout the centuries, the Orthodox liturgy has been richly embellished with cycles of hymns from a wide variety of sources. In the early centuries of the church, Christians sang in unison. The music was never written down but simply transmitted orally. It was not until the third century that a system of church melodies was put together. The use of instruments in Christian worship was discouraged by the early church fathers, as they felt that the instruments distracted the mind from thoughts of God and turned them toward the self. The Book of Psalms played a central role in early Christian worship, and in the East, the method of chanting the psalms was well established by the end of the fourth century.

Eastern Orthodox nuns singing a hymn in celebration of a special occasion.

MONASTERIES

As in the rest of Eastern Europe, monasteries play a vital role in Moldova. Apart from their purely spiritual work, they are major centers of education. In particular, monasteries have recorded in their chronicles all the major historical events. They have also translated various theological, historical, and literary works into the Romanian language.

Capriana, 22 miles (35 km) northwest of Chisinau, is the site of a celebrated 14th-century monastery. It lies amid the hills and is the most charming monastery in the countryside. Next to the old monastery, which has silver towers reaching to the high dome, is a new church with beautiful paintings that are slowly being restored. There is another famous monastery at Saharna, which is north of the capital and located on the Dniester River. This monastery is built underground. Cave Monastery, 31 miles (50 km) north of Chisinau, is near the Raut River. Built in the 15th century within a stony mound, this site had great tactical advantages and was used by Stephen the Great.

The Capriana Monastery is one of the most celebrated landmarks of modern Moldova.

LANGUAGE

A girl enjoys reading the many
local and classic novels.

THE MOLDOVAN LANGUAGE is a symbol of national pride and cultural heritage. It was suppressed during Soviet rule, but now that the country is independent, just about everyone speaks Moldovan. Another language spoken in Moldova is Romanian.

People who speak Romanian are able to understand Moldovan, and many consider the two to be essentially the same. Russian is the third major language, used for interethnic communication. For centuries, when Moldova was part of the Russian Empire, Russian was the official means of communication. Another language is that spoken by the Gagauz people. There are also local dialects heard in rural parts of the country.

Moldovan women enjoying a good chat.

The people of Moldova are exceedingly multilingual, to one degree or another. This is because of the country's complex political and social history. Like many other regions of dissolved empires, Moldova is distinctively multiethnic in character. It is this historical complexity that has created an ambiguity in the identity of its people. National and language identities have been hotly disputed and contested in all nation-building debates.

DEVELOPMENT OF MOLDOVAN

The Moldovan language can be traced back to Roman times. When the present-day Romanian and Moldavian territories were conquered by the Romans, the people living there had to adapt to the Roman language and culture. No script existed for "Romanian," the spoken language. The only written languages used in that region were Latin and Old Slavic, but at that time only a few privileged people, such as clerics, scholars, and some noblemen, were able to understand Latin or Old Slavic.

An ancient Cyrillic manuscript.

The first known manuscript in the Romanian language appeared in 1420, although it was still written in the Cyrillic characters used for Old Slavic. The actual development of the Romanian written script began in the 16th century. At that time, merchants and craftsmen needed a means of written communication to record their trade transactions without being obliged to learn Latin or Old Slavic, and so the Romanian written language was adopted. The written form of the Moldavian language developed later. Today, with its Latin script, Moldavian is basically the same as Romanian. The only difference is in the phonetics and vocabulary. As Moldova once belonged to Romania, this similarity is easy to understand.

LANGUAGE POLICY FROM 1812 TO 1917

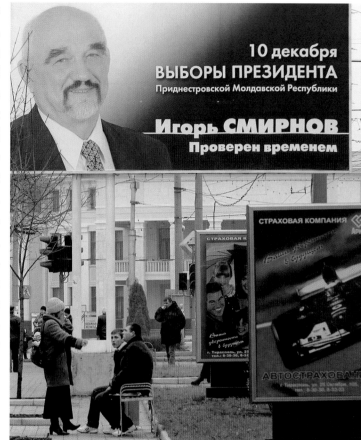

Moldovan language signboards adorn this park in **Bender**, **Transnistria**.

In 1812 Moldavia became part of the Russian Empire. The first Romanian school in Moldavia was established by Gheorghe Asachi, who also edited the first Romanian newspaper. In official documents, Moldavian was declared the second national language. Russian was the first national language.

When Czar Alexander I died in 1825 and Nicholas I came to the throne, the Moldavian people slowly lost their privileges, including their language rights. In 1828 their autonomous status was removed; Moldavians occupying posts in administration were replaced by Russians; the Russian legal and administrative systems were introduced; and Romanian schools were closed. From then until the Russian Revolution in 1917, Romanian could be spoken only in private areas. To pursue a career, knowledge of Russian was indispensable.

LANGUAGE IN THE MOLDAVIAN SOCIALIST SOVIET REPUBLIC

From 1917 until Lenin's death in 1924, the country enjoyed a tolerant nationalistic language policy. All ethnic groups had equal rights, and some even received privileges. Their native languages and cultures were promoted, linguists developed written forms of the spoken minority languages, and school lessons were conducted in native languages.

When Stalin came to power, he replaced non-Russians and nonconformist Russians in government, administration, and other public positions with his Russian supporters. Russian became the local language, and learning it in school became compulsory. To improve one's social status, one had to learn Russian and adapt to Russian culture. The main aim of Stalin's policy was to deny that Moldavians and Romanians had been one people.

After Stalin's death in 1953, Khrushchev relaxed these policies, and it became possible again to take part in the cultural life of Romania. Romanian books were sold, and Romanian films were shown. There were even exchange programs organized between Moldavian and Romanian students, enterprises, and theaters.

In the mid-1960s, however, the situation worsened. An anti-Romanian campaign was started, and an emphasis was placed on the independence of Moldavia from Romania. Authors were criticized for Romanian language

Young Moldovan boys learning Russian in school.

influences, and Romanian books and films were prohibited from use. Exchange programs were also no longer possible. By the 1970s, the situation improved slightly.

When Gorbachev became leader of the USSR in 1985, he implemented a policy of glasnost and perestroika, or restructuring. This encouraged a public opposition movement consisting mainly of writers and linguists who criticized the language policies of the past. In 1988 the Alexe Mateevici Cultural Club was founded. Mateevici, an Orthodox priest who died in 1917, had written a poem entitled "Limba noastra" ("Our Language"). The main demand of this movement and other opposition groups was the promotion of an accurate interpretation of the Moldavian language and history. The protestors campaigned for increased visibility for Moldovan cultural features in public life, abolishment of mixed schools, and the establishment of separate schools for each nation. Mixed schools had parallel classes: Moldavian-Russian, Russian-Ukrainian, and Russian-Bulgarian. During final discussions in parliament, 500,000 people demonstrated on behalf of the Mateevici movement.

Women sharing a joke. Many of the older generation Moldovans speak Russian.

Two laws were finally passed in August 1989 to revise the language policy and stress the independence of the Moldovan and Russian cultures. Moldavian, using the Cyrillic script, was declared the state language to be used in political, economic, social, and cultural life. The intrinsic connection between the Romanian and Moldavian languages was officially recognized. Gagauz became the second state language in areas with a high proportion of Gagauz people, and Russian became the language of communication among the different nationalities. After independence, Moldovans debated whether the name of their language should be changed from *Moldavian* to *Moldovan*. The president explained that *Moldovan* was used in the constitution for political reasons—to lessen the fears of those who opposed imminent reunification with Romania. The public response to the change in name was a resounding yes.

USE OF RUSSIAN BEFORE INDEPENDENCE

The rural population living in villages hardly had any contact with Russians, so there was no need for them to use Russian, which they learned at school. An exception was Moldovan men who had to do military service, since Russian was the only official language used by the Red Army, where people of different nationalities served together.

For the urban population, which had a high proportion of non-Moldovans, Russian was a common language. Until 1991, it was the language of everyday life. Speaking Russian in public was unavoidable for the urban population. Even today, most urban Moldovans are familiar with Russian.

THE MEDIA

Many ethnic
Russians have had
to leave Moldova
where they have
lived all their lives
as the different
language and
different alphabet
make life just
too difficult.

Moldova's media industry has grown in the past decade. By 2009 there were 37 terrestrial channels, 47 radio stations, seven major newspapers, and 168 cable operators. The press is generally divided into pro-government or opposition party leanings, and political parties are free to publish their own titles.

The government does not restrict foreign publications. Such publications do not have a wide circulation, however, since they are very expensive by local standards. Russian newspapers are available, and some of them publish a special Moldovan weekly supplement. Moldovan editions of Russian newspapers are among the best-selling publications in the country. However, the reach and impact of print media are low.

While press freedom is protected by the Moldovan constitution, the penal code and press laws prohibit defamation and insulting the state. Reporters Without Borders (Reporters sans frontières, or RSF) has reported that the media were particularly targeted by demonstrators and "treated as an enemy" by government forces during the postelection protests that took place in April 2009.

The OSCE mission to Moldova closely observes the media situation in Moldova, including the Transnistrian region. The media climate in Transnistria remains restrictive. Authorities continue their ongoing campaign to silence independent opposition voices and movements by applying administrative pressure on independent local newspapers and placing restrictions on other media.

Television is by far the most popular medium in Moldova. The most popular channel, Moldova 1, is available nationwide and is operated by public broadcaster Teleradio Moldova. Media critics say the station tends to lean toward a pro-government slant. In addition, Russia's Channel 1 and Romania's Atena 1 are widely available. Pro TV is Chisinau's independent network. The authorities in the autonomous Transnistria region operate their own TV and radio stations.

A supplementary edition of the government newspaper, *Independent Moldova*. It is published in Russian and Moldovan.

ARTS

A woman plays the kobesa in her traditional costume.
Many Moldovans are artistically and musically inclined.

F ROM A CULTURAL PERSPECTIVE, Moldova is a fascinating country. Theater, opera, dance, and music are Moldova's main performing arts. Visual arts are most evident in churches with their impressive frescoes. Traditional crafts, such as carving and embroidery, are also thriving.

Market stall selling Russian dolls along a street in Chisinau.

A traditional music group performing in a park.

CULTURAL TRADITIONS

Moldova's cultural traditions, influenced primarily by Romania, can be traced back to the period of Roman colonization in the second century A.D. After the Roman withdrawal in A.D. 271, Moldova and Romania were influenced by the Byzantine Empire and later the Ottoman Turks. By the 14th century, however, a Moldovan identity began to emerge, although the people retained close cultural links with Romanian groups. Eastern Moldovans were also influenced by Slavic culture from neighboring Ukraine.

FOLK CULTURE

Moldova's folk culture is extremely rich; "Miorita" and "Meserul Manole" are popular ancient folk songs that play a tremendous role in the traditional culture of Moldova.

Soviet rule resulted in many ethnic Romanian intellectuals leaving the country to avoid being killed or deported during and after World War II. With their departure, Romanian cultural influences diminished. Soviet authorities developed cultural and scientific centers and institutions that were filled with Russians and other non-Romanian ethnic groups. The rural, ethnic Romanian population was allowed to express itself only in folklore and folk art. Although folk arts flourished, any that showed Romanian cultural influence were destroyed by the Soviets. For instance, the Romanian moccasin was

VALENTIN KORYAKIN was born in 1933 in Siberia. He graduated from the Belarusian Theater Art Institute in 1966. A member of the Union of Artists of Moldova since 1969, Koryakin has had his work exhibited at many prestigious international exhibitions in countries such as France, Germany, Switzerland, Russia, and Belarus. Some of his more famous pieces are preserved in museums in Chisinau and other cities throughout Eastern Europe. They are also owned by private collectors in the United States, Israel, Japan, and Canada.

VITALIY TISEEV was born in 1935 in Moldova and studied at the Ilya Repin Art College in Chisinau from 1959 to 1964. In his professional career, he has produced a series of paintings devoted to Moldova. His work is sold to art galleries, museums, and private collectors throughout the art world in Europe, the United States, Canada, Israel, and India. His works have also been published in many magazines and books. His daughter Tatiana and son Sergey are also painters.

Other important artists are Dmitriy Kharin, Anna Ravliuk, and Mihai Brunea, who is the vice president of the Union of Artists of Moldova.

replaced by the Russian boot. Since independence, the moccasin has been brought back.

Folk traditions, including ceramics and weaving, continue to be practiced in rural areas. Handmade wool rugs, glass, intricate wood carvings, earth-colored and black pottery pieces, native dress, tablecloths, wooden boxes, and dolls are some examples of the traditional crafts still produced today in Moldova.

PAINTING

Moldova's artists have never enjoyed a worldwide reputation, neither in the past nor in contemporary times. Several have achieved some success outside of Moldova, however.

The ornate interior and ceiling frescoes of the Capriana Monastery.

CHURCH FRESCOES

A fresco is a painting done with water-based pigments on a wall or a ceiling while the plaster is still wet. Frescoes adorn churches in Moldova and are examples of art that portray life in the Middle Ages. Some of the monasteries also have painted exterior walls that date from the 15th and 16th centuries. Most of them depict saints and the possible punishments or rewards awaiting the faithful in the next life.

MUSIC

Moldova has about 110 music and fine arts schools from 32 regions. The S. Rachmaninoff and Ciprian Porumbescu music schools are prestigious places to study and have contributed greatly to Moldova's musical traditions. Composer Yevgeni Doga, a Moldovan, is well known in Eastern Europe. The Moldovan Academy Ensemble has performed in European and international competitions and has won many awards for its chamber concerts and renditions of native folk music. The Academy of Music in Chisinau is one of Eastern Europe's oldest and most distinguished conservatories. Graduates play in the finest symphonies and chamber orchestras in Europe and the United States.

The National Philharmonic Society travels widely to other European countries to perform and is held in high regard everywhere it is heard. Its interpretation of Ludwig van Beethoven's Symphony No. 9, often performed with the Doina Choir, is very popular among classical music enthusiasts. The orchestra has repeatedly performed this magnificent piece at many concerts. Another performance that delights Moldovans is Brahms's Symphony No. 1. When playing at home, the Moldovan Philharmonic frequently invites Romanian musicians to join them, providing an opportunity for promising young musicians to conduct their symphonic orchestra.

Another well-known Moldovan singer is Nelly Ciobanu. A winner of multiple international competitions, Ciobanu represented Moldova in the 2009 Eurovision Song Contest.

Dressed in the traditional Moldovan outfit, Nelly Ciobanu sings her song "Hora din Moldova" ("Dance From Moldova") at the 2009 Eurovision Song Contest.

MONUMENTS AND STATUES

Along the main boulevard in Chisinau is a statue of Grigory Kotovski. In the 1920s Kotovski attacked Romania in a series of raids. Today some Moldovans see him as a Moldovan Robin Hood, whereas others consider him a bandit.

Stalinist blocks and neoclassical buildings can be found along the capital's main boulevard. On one corner of the Piata Marii Adunari Nationale stands the statue of the legendary Stefan cel Mare, or Stephen the Great, the Romanian prince and national hero. This statue, which was made in 1928, had to be moved several times during World War II to save it from falling into enemy hands. Under Soviet rule, it was transported to a more obscure place in the park. In the 1940s the Soviets replaced it with a statue of Lenin. After independence, the statue was brought back to its initial location. In front of the History Museum is a statue of a female wolf, feeding the two founders of Rome, Romulus and Remus. This serves as a reminder of the country's Latin ancestors.

A statue of a female wolf feeding Romulus and Remus stands in front of the History Museum in Chisinau today.

A FAMOUS MONUMENT

In spring 1999, more than 1,000 people attended the unveiling ceremony of a monument to Moldova's most beloved ballad singers, Ion and Doina Aldea-Teodorovici, who were killed in a car accident in neighboring Romania in October 1992. The couple were known as promoters of the national cause. Ion Aldea-Teodorovici, composer and singer, was born in 1954 in southern Moldova. Doina, his wife and band partner, was born in 1958 in Chisinau. The peak of their careers came in 1989 to 1992, when Moldova gained its independence.

The bronze monument stands near the national university. Local sculptor Iurie Canasin, architect Nico Zaporojan, and businessman Anatol Josanu, who financed the project, worked together in partnership. The ceremony was attended by then-president Petru Lucinschi, various officials, the couple's parents and son, artists, composers, singers, businesspeople, and students, all of whom laid flowers at the memorial.

THEATER

Moldova has 12 professional theaters. Most of them perform in Romanian. Chisinau offers the most choices for theatergoers, but there are many small theaters outside of the capital. Members of ethnic minorities manage a number of folklore groups and amateur theaters throughout the country.

At the major theaters, performances are in Moldovan, except at the Chekhov Drama Theater in Chisinau and the Russian Drama Theater in Tiraspol, both of which perform solely in Russian. The Licurici Republic Puppet Theater in Chisinau performs in both Romanian and Russian.

The National Palace Theater with its stylish Corinthian columns and orange facade has shows throughout the year, although the month of March

A drama theater and dance group performing a well-loved Moldovan folk tale.

marks the start of traditional music and dance. Apart from the National Palace Theater, the Opera and Ballet Theater is a great place to hear piano and organ concerts and musical performances by local and visiting guests.

There are also a variety of other theaters—Satiricus, Ginta Latina, Luceafarul, Eugene Ionesco, and Mateevici. Theater tours to the United States by the highly regarded Ionesco Theater troupe performing classical plays are common. The Chisinau Marionette Theater opens its theatrical season in February.

LITERARY TRADITIONS

The oldest original Moldavian manuscript still exists. It was written in 1429. Elaborately authored and illustrated books and manuscripts were produced in monasteries during the 13th and 14th centuries. They were extremely expensive to produce at that time. When the printing press became common, making books became easier and cheaper. Today book exhibitions encourage literary exchange and introduce the younger generations to well-known writers of the past. One such exhibition is the 10-day Mihai Eminescu Memorial Days.

MIHAI EMINESCU

Mihai Eminescu represents the pinnacle of Romanian and Moldovan literature and poetry. A national poet in both countries, he wrote poems that evoke beautifully the nature and soul of the people. In his work, all the national characteristics come to life. His poems combine his thoughts, sensibility, and creativity.

Eminescu was born in 1850. By 1866 he had published his first poem, signed with his real name, M. Eminoviciu. Joining the National Theater, he met Veronica Micle, who became the great love of his life. He held a number of jobs but continued to write and publish his poetry until he fell ill in 1884. He died in 1889. Here is one of his poems:

WHAT IS LOVE?

*What is love? A lifetime spent
Of days that pain does fill,
That thousand tears can't content,
But asks for tears still.
With but a little glance coquet
Your soul it knows to tie,
That of its spell you can't forget
Until the day you die.
Upon your threshold does it stand,
In every nook conspire,
That you may whisper hand in hand
Your tale of heart's aspire.
Till fades the very earth and sky,
Your heart completely broken,
And all the world hangs on a sigh,
A word but partly spoken.*

*It follows you for weeks and weeks
And in your soul assembles
The memory of blushing cheeks
And eyelash fair that trembles.
It comes to you a sudden ray
As though of starlight's spending,
How many and many a time each day
And every night unending.
For of your life has fate decreed
That pain shall it enfold,
As does the clinging waterweed
About a swimmer hold.*

(English translation by Corneliu M. Popescu)

LEISURE

A man dressed in Soviet army uniform plays an accordion on a street in downtown Chisinau.

LEISURE PURSUITS IN MOLDOVA are varied. In rural areas, activities tend to center around village life. On weekends, urban Moldovans attend the theater and concerts. For young people working in the cities, weekends provide an opportunity for them to return to their parents' home for a visit.

Old men playing chess on a park bench in Chisinau.

Chisinau has a wonderful circus run by the government. Performances are held in a giant circular-domed building. The circus has 158 staff. Performing animals, acrobats, and clowns entertain the crowd. Traveling circuses, such as those from China and Russia, are also hosted here.

RELAXING AT HOME

Moldovans love to invite friends and family home for a meal. Friends often stop by a person's house without prior notice, and the reception is always friendly. Sometimes even strangers are welcomed into Moldovan homes. When friends gather, they like to play board games as a way of passing time. Board games also have the advantage of involving the entire family. Among the games, chess is the most popular.

On weekdays, after work, most people spend their time watching television or a movie video. In the past there were few program choices, and much of it was for propaganda purposes. Now people have more choices on the main television channels. Listening to the radio is also a popular pastime. Despite an increase in television viewers, this form of entertainment has managed to keep its audience.

With more than 500 daily, weekly, and monthly newspapers and magazines in Moldova, reading newspapers and magazines is a common activity and a popular form of relaxation after a busy day at work.

The Bulevardul Stefan cel Mare opera and ballet theater in Chisinau.

CONCERTS AND THEATER

Attending music concerts, whether rock, classical, or folk, and watching plays are popular forms of entertainment for Moldovans. The numerous musical events are a legacy from the Soviets, who frequently had musicians and singers perform in the various factories as a means of keeping the workers happy and satisfied. With enormous government subsidies for the arts, going to the theater was an affordable outing in the Soviet days. Unfortunately such financial support has now been drastically reduced, and market forces are slowly being introduced. The result is a significant decline in concert attendance because few people can afford the high ticket prices.

Moviegoing used to be a favorite activity among younger Moldovans, since there are many movies in Moldovan and Russian, as well as Hollywood films featuring their favorite movie stars. However, as home videos become cheaper and more accessible to the general public, the cinema is slowly losing its audience.

OUTDOOR PURSUITS

Moldova's climate is ideal for outdoor activities, as the summers are never too hot, rainfall is sparse, and the winters are short compared with those of other countries in this part of the world. The terrain is limited, with no sandy beaches to play ball on or mountains to climb. Nevertheless, walking in the parks in towns and cities can be very relaxing, and exploring the countryside, coupled with a family picnic by a lake, is a pleasant way to spend the weekend.

Hiking in the heavily forested Codri Hills is an experience that Moldovans especially enjoy in the spring and the fall. The advantage of a small country is that such rural areas are easily accessible to city dwellers.

A family hiking in the Codri Hills, site of the country's nature reserve.

RURAL ACTIVITIES

Under the Soviet system, free time for young people was strictly monitored, especially in the cities. It was important for them to be doing something productive all the time, such as playing the piano, going to music school, or participating in sports, such as wrestling or weight lifting. Leisure in the rural parts of the country, however, was more relaxed, and children could do what they like. Leisure activities have not changed much since independence and are still conducted along traditional gender lines. Men occupy their free time with wood carving and perhaps some furniture-making. They may gather in a group while engaging in such activities, so there is a fair amount of chatter and gossip.

Women spend their free time doing embroidery or making dresses and quilts, as being idle is frowned on. These activities are carried out in a group setting, so talking and sharing a joke are part of the enjoyment. Passing on traditional stories that have a moral by word of mouth to younger members of the community is prevalent throughout the countryside. Children love these stories, and it helps to connect them with the history and traditions of their motherland.

SPORTS

Football, as soccer is called there, is unsurpassed as the national sport in Moldova. It is popular with young and old alike and is actively promoted in school. In the evenings, a group of young men can typically be found playing a friendly game or simply kicking a ball around. Competition is fierce between Chisinau's two top teams, FC Sheriff and FC Zimbru. Teams at the grassroots level, on the other hand, find it a lot harder to survive. Young players are often forced to give up the sport at an early age because of a lack of funding.

Palaces of Culture are popular sports recreation centers for children. Many sports and activities are available to meet different interests, such as soccer, tennis, swimming, judo, karate, and—for the more intellectual—chess. In Soviet times, these social centers or clubs were owned by the government, but they are now privately owned and much more expensive, so the number of people using the facilities has dropped.

Tennis is popular in Moldova, and the Specialized Sport School in Chisinau has produced some excellent players who have done well in national and international competitions.

Local children learning karate in Moldova.

FESTIVALS

A colorful dancer performs at a festival in Moldova.

MOLDOVA HAS RELIGIOUS holidays, pagan festivals, and celebrations for national events. Since many people still live in the rural countryside, the celebration of traditional festivals continues to survive. There are also many established music and dance festivals.

Priests in procession during a religious festival in Moldova.

Two Moldovan girls playing in the Saint Lazar cemetery in Chisinau. It is customary for Moldavians to visit the cemeteries and take care of their relatives' graves on Easter.

NEW YEAR'S DAY

Unlike Americans, Moldovans do not hold large-scale, public New Year's Eve parties to usher in the new year. The most common celebration is having friends and family sit down together for a special meal and champagne. After the meal everyone gathers around the television to watch the countdown to midnight. On New Year's Day children go door-to-door with songs and poems. It is customary to give them small amounts of money or candy.

EASTER

Easter was not an officially celebrated holiday when Moldova was part of the Soviet Union. Nevertheless, it has always been an important religious event for Moldovans. The celebrations start with Palm Sunday, the Sunday before Easter, which honors the day Jesus rode into Jerusalem on a donkey. On this day, palm leaves are hung in churches and homes. The following Friday, Good Friday, marks the day of the Crucifixion, and Easter Sunday is a day of joy for Christians because it celebrates Jesus rising from the dead and, after 40 days, ascending to heaven. On the following day, Easter Monday, people visit and pray at the graves of loved ones. This ritual symbolizes the hope that their family members have gone to heaven just as Jesus did.

In the Orthodox Church, Easter is usually celebrated about three to four weeks later than Easter in the West. On the Orthodox clerical calendar, Easter usually falls in April.

CHRISTMAS

When Moldova was part of the Soviet Union, Christmas was not openly celebrated or officially acknowledged. However, it provided Moldovans with an opportunity to make merry and feast, and a huge family celebration was usually held.

The festive season begins with Saint Nicholas's Day on December 6, when preparations for the big event officially start. Any special food that needs to be prepared ahead for Christmas would be made at this time. Shopping for new clothes, materials to make new clothes, or presents is a major activity for Moldovans.

Santa Clauses celebrating Christmas. This happy occasion is not complete without his presence.

Celebrating the Festival of the Transfiguration in church.

Between December 6 and the end of the month, there are traditional practices that represent the end of one year and the approach of a new one. One such custom in the countryside is the pulling of a plow through a residential area to symbolize the cutting of a furrow. This is believed to bring prosperity to the people living there. The plow is decorated with leaves, which represent fertility and growth.

Christmas Eve and Christmas Day, which fall on December 24 and 25, are spent with family members. There is generally a lot of eating and drinking, and everyone has a wonderful time. It is customary for families to gather together for a festive meal. Going to church on Christmas is an important activity. It reminds people that the true meaning of the holiday is the birth of Christ.

FESTIVAL OF THE TRANSFIGURATION

This festival, which takes place in August, commemorates the day when Jesus Christ took three of his disciples, Peter, James, and John, up to a mountain where Moses and Elijah appeared. According to the Gospels, Jesus was transfigured on this day—his face and clothes became white and shining.

In the Orthodox Church, the Festival of the Transfiguration has always been a major festival. It celebrates the revelation of the eternal glory of the Second Person of the Trinity, which was normally veiled during Christ's life on earth. It is not known when the festival was first celebrated, but it was observed in Jerusalem as early as the seventh century and in most parts of the Byzantine Empire by the ninth century.

SECULAR HOLIDAYS

On March 8, in honor of International Women's Day, gifts of candy and flowers are given to women. The intent of the holiday is similar to Saint Valentine's Day, but romance is not necessarily present. Gifts are meant to be small and inexpensive and represent friendship and best wishes for the future.

May 1 was a major event before independence. There were military marches and parades in honor of the workers, and local officials made public speeches. It is still a holiday today, although the military marches have all but disappeared. Moldovans now take the opportunity to go to the countryside, have a picnic, and enjoy the lovely spring weather after a long, dreary winter.

Soldiers marching at a military parade during the Independence Day celebration in Moldova.

A Moldovan dance troupe performing during the spring festival.

SPRING FESTIVAL

The month of March marks the start of Martisor, Moldova's spring festival. The festival marks the rebirth of nature after winter. During this lively festival, classical and folk music predominate. Many special concerts and cultural events are held during Martisor.

The International Music Festival of Martisor is attended by bands and artistes from 17 countries, including the United States, France, Germany, Russia, Romania, and Ukraine. Concerts are held not only in Chisinau but also in all of Moldova's other districts. The festival usually opens with a performance focusing on traditional spring customs. Additional concerts are hosted by the Organ Hall, the National Opera, and the National Philharmonic.

The festival occurs during the time when the traditional custom of honoring women is observed throughout the country. The music festival includes an exclusive performance for women, scheduled on International Women's Day. It is attended by Moldovan musicians and fashion houses. Flowers and small gifts are given to all women and girls.

There are a small number of Jews in Moldova, and they celebrate a few Jewish festivals. The Jewish holiday of Rosh Hashanah, usually celebrated in September, has a fourfold meaning: It is the beginning of a new year on the Jewish calendar as well as the Day of Judgment, the Day of Remembrance, and the Day of Shofar Blowing. On the Day of Judgment, Jews across the world examine their past deeds and ask for forgiveness for their sins. On the Day of Remembrance, the Jews review the history of their people and pray for Israel. On the Day of Shofar Blowing, the shofar, or ram's horn, is blown in the temple to herald the beginning of the 10-day period known as the High Holidays, which ends with Yom Kippur, the Day of Atonement and the most sacred of the Jewish holidays.

Passover commemorates the time when the Israelites were enslaved by the Egyptians, around 3,000 years ago. According to the Book of Exodus, Moses, a Jewish shepherd, was instructed by God to warn the pharaoh that God would severely punish Egypt if the Israelites were not freed. The pharaoh ignored Moses' request. In response, God unleashed a series of 10 terrible plagues on the people of Egypt. When the pharaoh agreed to free the Israelites, his army chased them through the desert toward the Red Sea. The waves of the Red Sea parted, and the Israelites were able to cross to the other side. As soon as they all reached the other side, the waves came together again, trapping the pharaoh's army.

FOOD

A vendor grills sausages at the
Pieta Centrala market in Chisinau.

ROMANIAN, RUSSIAN, Ukrainian, and Bulgarian cuisines are all part of the Moldovan diet. Garlic, onions, and herbs are used in the cooking of many dishes. Meat, bread, potatoes, and vegetables are staples for the main meal. Because fresh produce can be expensive for the average Moldovan, many city dwellers grow their own food in small gardens outside of town or in the countryside.

The locals enjoy drinking tea at cafés such as these in Moldova.

A typical Moldovan meal consists of meats, home made breads, cold cuts, and wine.

A SOCIAL OCCASION

Eating in Moldova is much more than simply consuming food to stay alive. Enjoyment of food in the company of others is paramount. The sharing of food as a group is an established and highly valued Moldovan custom. It is customary when visiting friends or family to have something to eat and drink. The host will be disappointed if the offer is refused. Casual dining is by far the norm.

The most common soup eaten at lunch is Ukrainian borscht, made of tomato juice and beets.

DAILY MEALS

Moldovans tend to get up early and have a light breakfast, usually some bread or pastry, and then have a hearty lunch. In urban areas breakfast usually consists of open sandwiches with sausage or cheese, coffee or tea, and fruit preserves. People in rural areas tend to eat a more substantial breakfast of kasha (hot porridge), potatoes, bread, and sheep's cheese.

Lunch is typically the main meal of the day, even for those who are working. An everyday meal begins with a choice of many soups, followed by a main dish of fried meat, baked chicken, or salted or pickled fish. Meat is an important part of the Moldovan diet. Smoked meats are sometimes eaten with fried potatoes and boiled vegetables as accompaniment.

Rice, stuffed cabbage, cucumbers, and tomato salad are also popular among Moldovans. Cheese is often served as a conclusion to the meal. Casseroles and other baked foods are the favorite foods of most people, appearing often on the daily menu of local restaurants. For dinner, people tend to eat only one course.

Bread is an important staple that is served with most meals; wine is served with lunch and dinner.

THE MOLDOVAN KITCHEN

A Moldovan kitchen is very similar to one in the United States, although there are not so many appliances. A coffeemaker would be an unusual item to find in a Moldovan kitchen, as coffee is made espresso style. An electric kettle, on the other hand, is indispensable. Preparing a meal, which is predominantly a woman's job, is time-consuming, as dishes are prepared from scratch. Popping a precooked meal into the microwave oven at the end of a hard day's work would be a luxury for the average Moldovan woman.

A woman preparing a salad to serve along with her freshly baked bread.

Except for salt, bay leaves, onions, and garlic, relatively few seasonings or spices are used in the flavoring of food. A lot of animal fat, oil, butter, and mayonnaise are used, and food is often fried.

FRESH PRODUCE

The rich soil and abundant rainfall in Moldova has resulted in ideal conditions for growing many kinds of vegetables and fruit. Cabbage, potatoes, carrots, beets, and turnips are common crops. In addition, there are tomatoes, peppers, zucchinis, cucumbers, eggplants, and lettuce.

There are plenty of orchards in the valleys of the Codri Hills. The orchards produce apples, plums, peaches, apricots, and walnuts. In fall the bark of the apple trees is wrapped with thick strips of cloth to protect the bark from being burned by the sun or eaten by animals. A greater variety of fruit, such as strawberries, cherries, watermelons, raspberries, and grapes, is available in the summer.

Farmers raise pigs, goats, poultry, and sheep throughout the country. Pigs in particular are plentiful, as pork is a popular dish.

Fresh vegetables being sold at the Pieta Centrala marketplace in Chisinau.

TRADITIONAL CUISINE

Mamaliga (mah-me-LI-ga), mashed cornmeal, is the national dish. Traditionally, *mamaliga* was made in a cast-iron kettle over an open fire and given to farmworkers as a cheap yet filling meal. People sometimes eat it cold for breakfast. Moldovans enjoy *mamaliga* when it is served with *ghiveci* (GHEE-vetch), a vegetable dish, and mushrooms sautéed in a wine and herb sauce.

Mititei (me-tee-TAY) are grilled meatballs made from pork mixed with beef or lamb. Usually cooked outdoors over charcoal, they are eaten as a snack or an appetizer and are sold by street vendors in the cities. *Mititei* are usually consumed with a glass of beer or wine.

Sarmale (sar-MALL-eh) consists of cabbage or grape leaves stuffed with rice, meat, and herbs. The filling can be cooked in tomato or lemon sauce. The finished product is often served with cream.

Borscht, a rich-tasting beet and vegetable soup, is a Ukrainian national dish that is a great favorite in Moldova. Yogurt is used to make its texture silky. *Ciorba* (CHOR-ba) is a sour-tasting soup that is traditionally made from the fermented juice of wheat bran. Lemon juice is now used as a substitute to make the sour base.

Moldovans frequent meat shops such as these in the city.

Brinza (BRIHN-zah), a cheese made from sheep's milk, is cured in brine. It is creamy, rich, and salty, ranging from soft and spreadable to semidry and crumbly.

Common desserts are *placinte* (pla-CHIN-te), which are similar to turnovers, and baklava, a Turkish pastry with crushed pistachios or almonds glazed with thick syrup. The result is an extremely rich and sweet dessert.

TRADITIONAL DRINKS

Homemade alcohol, although illegal, is still prepared in parts of the country. It is extremely potent and certainly an acquired taste. Wine and beer are more popular and are legally available. Moldova is well known for its fine cognac and brandy.

Tea is widely consumed, but Turkish-style coffee is far more common. It is usually drunk black, served in small cups, and is very strong and sweet. Water or sometimes milk accompanies daily meals. Lemonade is a popular choice to quench one's thirst.

An assortment of popular Moldovan desserts are often served to guests.

Wine from the famous winery of Cricova in Moldova.

WINE

Moldova is one of the most interesting wine areas in Europe, with great potential for growth. Wine has been made in this area since the seventh century B.C. Moldova lies on the same latitude as the greatest wine-producing country, France, although its wine production is much smaller.

Moldovan wines were used by the Soviet Union as a source of cheap and readily available alcohol. Today the focus is on improving the quality of the wine rather than producing it in mass quantities. The very best wine is pressed and kept in oak barrels for many years.

RESTAURANTS

Most local restaurants in the main cities serve a basic meal that costs much less than a meal in a Western restaurant. Chisinau has some restaurants with beautiful interiors. Dinner at these formal dining places is more expensive. Some of them have music performances during dinner hours.

There are many ethnic restaurants in Chisinau offering Indian, Mexican, Korean, Chinese, Jewish, and Italian cuisine. Fast-food restaurants sell hamburgers, fries, and pizza. Outside of lunch during the working day, eating out is uncommon for the average Moldovan.

GHIVECI (ROMANIAN VEGETABLE STEW)

4 servings

2 potatoes, quartered and sliced

½ head cauliflower, separated into florets

½ eggplant, cubed

2 carrots, sliced

1 small green or yellow summer squash, sliced

2 medium-size onions, quartered and sliced

½ cup (125 ml) green peas

½ cup (125 ml) green beans, cut

1 medium-size green or red bell pepper, seeded and cut in chunks

2 ribs celery, sliced

2 cups (500 ml) plum tomatoes with liquid

1½ cups (375 ml) vegetable bouillon

½ cup (125 ml) pure olive oil

2 cloves garlic, chopped

Salt and ground black pepper to taste

½ cup (125 ml) fresh dill and parsley, chopped

- Preheat oven to 350°F (180°C).
- Place the potatoes, cauliflower, eggplant, carrots, summer squash, onions, green peas, green beans, pepper, and celery in a three- or four-quart ungreased casserole dish.
- Pour the tomatoes on top.
- Mix the bouillon, olive oil, and garlic, then pour this mixture over the vegetables.
- Season with salt and pepper to taste, and stir once or twice.
- Sprinkle the dill and parsley on top.
- Cover the casserole dish and bake at least one hour or until the vegetables are of desired tenderness.
- Allow to cool a bit before serving over rice or *mamaliga*.

MOLDOVAN CORN AND FETA CHEESE BREAD

1 loaf

½ cup (125 ml) sour cream

2 large eggs, lightly beaten

2 cups (500 ml) milk

¾ cup (180 ml) unbleached,
    all-purpose flour

2 tsp (10 ml) baking powder

½ tsp (2.5 ml) baking soda

2 cups (500 ml) yellow cornmeal

½ tsp (2.5 ml) sugar

6 tbsp (90 ml) unsalted butter,
    melted and cooled

2 cups (500 ml) feta cheese,
    crumbled

- Preheat the oven to 350°F (180°C),
  then butter a 13 x 9 inch rectangular
  loaf pan.

- In a large bowl, combine the sour
  cream, eggs, and milk then set aside.

- Sift the flour, baking powder, and
  baking soda into a separate bowl,
  then stir in the cornmeal and sugar.
  Pour this mixture into the large bowl.

- Add butter and stir the mixture well
  to combine.

- Add the feta cheese and blend well.

- Transfer the mixture into the
  prepared pan and bake in middle
  rack of the oven for about 35 to 40
  minutes, or until well risen, light
  golden brown, and firm to the touch.

- Allow to cool in the tin for 5 minutes,
  then transfer to a wire rack to cool
  completely before serving.

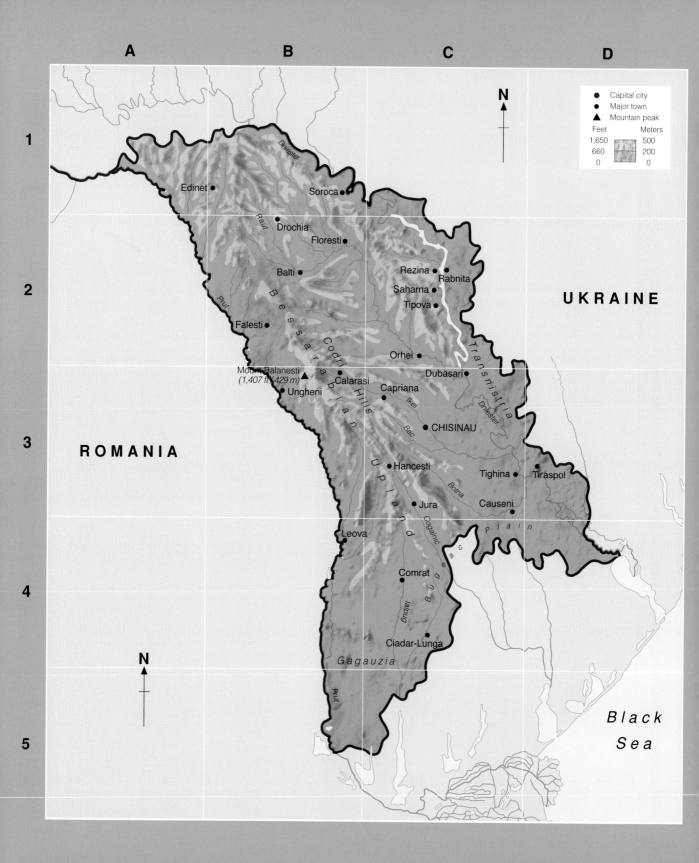

MAP OF MOLDOVA

ECONOMIC MOLDOVA

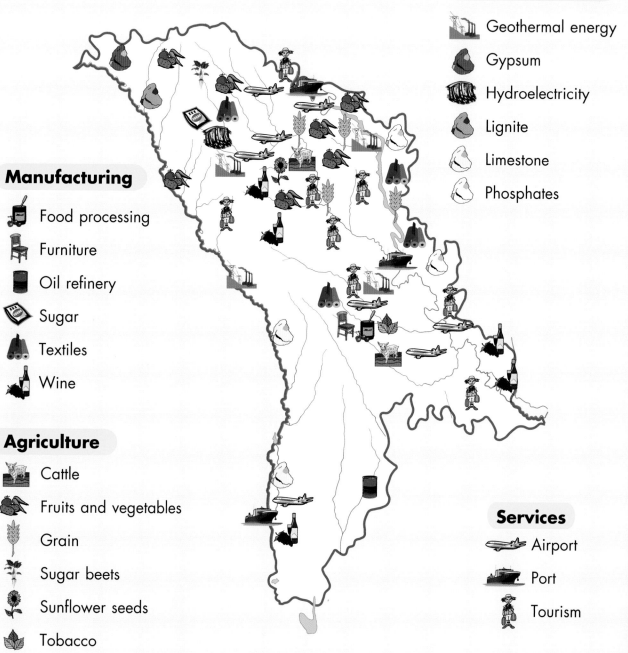

Natural Resources

- Geothermal energy
- Gypsum
- Hydroelectricity
- Lignite
- Limestone
- Phosphates

Manufacturing

- Food processing
- Furniture
- Oil refinery
- Sugar
- Textiles
- Wine

Agriculture

- Cattle
- Fruits and vegetables
- Grain
- Sugar beets
- Sunflower seeds
- Tobacco

Services

- Airport
- Port
- Tourism

ABOUT THE ECONOMY

OVERVIEW

Moldova is a small and sunny country, blessed with an abundance of arable land and a thriving agricultural industry. However, it is one of the poorest nations in Europe, with about 29.5 percent of its people living below the poverty line. The World Bank estimated Moldova's per capita gross national income of $3,210 in 2008 to be the lowest in Europe. Living standards are poor for the great majority of Moldovans, particularly in rural areas. In 2008, the average monthly wage was $228.15. More than a quarter of Moldova's economically active population work abroad. Remittances from those working abroad amounted to 38.3 percent of the gross domestic product (GDP) in 2008. Agriculture, especially wine, tobacco, and fruit, play a vital role in the economy, accounting for 40 percent of GDP. Most of Moldova's industry is located in Transnistria, which has a population of 533,000.

GROSS DOMESTIC PRODUCT (GDP)

$10.21 billion (2009 estimate)

GDP PER CAPITA

$2,400 (2009 estimate)

CURRENCY

Moldovan leu (plural lei), 1 leu = 100 bani
US$1 = 12.21 lei (2009 estimate)

LABOR FORCE

1,336,000 (2009 estimate)

LABOR FORCE BY SECTOR

Agriculture: 40.6 percent
Industry: 16 percent
Services: 43.3 percent (2006 estimate)

UNEMPLOYMENT RATE

2.6 percent (2009 estimate)

NATURAL RESOURCES

Lignite, phosphates, gypsum, limestone

AGRICULTURE

Vegetables, fruits, wine and spirits, grain, sugar beets, sunflower seeds, meat, milk, eggs, tobacco, walnuts

MAIN INDUSTRIES

Food processing, metal processing, machinery, textiles, clothing, footwear, hosiery, foundry equipment, refrigerators and freezers, washing machines

MAIN EXPORTS

Foodstuffs, wine, tobacco, textiles, clothing, footwear, machinery

MAIN IMPORTS

Oil, gas, coal, steel, machinery, foodstuffs, automobiles, chemical products, other consumer durables

MAJOR TRADING PARTNERS

Ukraine, Russia, Romania, Germany, Italy, Belarus, China

CULTURAL MOLDOVA

Soroca Fortress
Soroca's ancient fortress is one of the finest fortresses presiding over the meandering Nistru River. For centuries its battlements and turrets defended Moldova against invasion from the east. In the medieval period the fortress was part of a huge Moldovan defensive system, which consisted of four fortresses on the Nistru River, two on the Danube, and another three in the northern part of the country. With this "stone belt of fortresses," the country's borders were well protected.

Orheiul Vechi (Old Orhei)
With its breathtaking scenery, this ancient archaeological complex is situated in the beautiful winding valley of the Raut River, between the villages of Trebujeni and Butuceni. The grand settlement dates back to the Middle Ages where due to its advantageous geographical position on the steep banks of the Raut, settlements sprang up as early as in the Paleolithic epoch. The vestiges of two medieval towns, a mosque, two mausoleums, a caravan-seraglio, and three ancient stone bathhouses of the Golden Horde period remain. Some of the monastery complexes, dating back to the ninth century are functional even today.

Tipova Village
Famous for its waterfalls and springs, as well as for its cave monasteries, which are the largest in Eastern Europe. One of the country's top attractions is a monastery built there in the 11th century. According to legend, the country's greatest ruler, Stefan the Great (ca. 1437–1504), married his wife, Maria Voichita, at this monastery. The natural beauty of Tipova also attracts visitors from all over the world. Its hills are heavily forested, and there are many beautiful scenic pathways and rivers such as the Nistru and the Tipova.

Codri Reserve
Declared a scientific nature reserve by the government in 1971, this highly protected 13,942-acre (5,642-ha) reserve is divided into three functional zones: a strictly protected zone, a buffer zone, and an intermediate zone. Often praised as a "natural museum," it is home to almost a thousand species of plants, some of which are close to extinction, and various species of rare birds are endemic wildlife. The main forest trees here are tall oaks.

Stefan cel Mare Park
Celebrating the great Moldovan leader who defended his people against invading armies in the 15th century, this park runs along a boulevard bearing his name. Its pièce de résistance is the bronze statue of Stefan cel Mare. With its lush greenery, this park and its fountain provide a picturesque backdrop for the locals to relax.

Assumption of the Virgin Mary Church
The exact date of the construction of the Assumption of the Virgin Mary Church in Causeni is unknown; however, it is believed to date back to 1455. Legend has it that the Tartars only permitted the construction of churches that were lower than the height of a soldier on his horse, accounting for the lower half of this church being buried beneath the earth. The church is about 50 miles (80 km) south of Chisinau and is the only one in all of Bessarabia that has wall frescoes.

Triumphal Arch
Standing in the heart of Chisinau's city center, this structure is a combination of Corinthian columns and other Greek and Roman styles. A giant copper bell is suspended from the arch's dome with chimes to sound the clock. Historically significant, the bell was cast in 1839 using metal the Russians had collected from defeating the Ottoman Turks, and signal the change of hands of Moldova from the Turks to the Russians.

Wine Regions (Milestii Mici and Cricova wineries)
The cultivation of wine is one of the most ancient activities of the Moldovan people. For connoisseurs of fine wine, a visit to the underground wine cellars of Milestii Mici and Cricova is a must. These cellars form the world's largest underground network of wine storage space, with as much as 37 miles (60 km) of limestone-walled roadways being dedicated to storing wines. It is also here that people can take a trip around the underground streets, which stretch for more than 62 miles (100 km).

ABOUT THE CULTURE

OFFICIAL NAME
Republic of Moldova

CAPITAL
Chisinau

MAJOR CITIES
Tiraspol, Balti, Tighina, Ungheni, Soroca, Orhei

NATIONAL FLAG
Three equal vertical bands of blue, yellow, and red; emblem is a Roman eagle, bearing a shield with a stylized ox head.

ADMINISTRATIVE DIVISIONS
Districts: Anenii Noi, Basarabeasca, Briceni, Cahul, Cantemir, Calarasi, Causeni, Cimislia, Criuleni, Donduseni, Drochia, Dubasari, Edinet, Falesti, Floresti, Glodeni, Hancesti, Ialoveni, Leova, Nisporeni, Ocnita, Orhei, Rezina, Riscani, Singerei, Soldanesti, Soroca, Stefan-Voda, Straseni, Taraklia, Telenesti, Ungheni
Municipalities: Balti, Bender, Chisinau
Autonomous territorial unit: Gagauzia
Territorial unit: Stinga Nistrului (Transnistria)

TOTAL AREA
13,070 square miles (33,851 square km)

HIGHEST POINT
Mount Balanesti (1,407 feet/429 m)

POPULATION
4,320,748 million (2009 estimate)

LIFE EXPECTANCY
Male: 65 years
Female: 72 years (2008 estimate)

BIRTHRATE
11.1 births per 1,000 population (2009 estimate)

DEATH RATE
10.8 deaths born per 1,000 population (2009 estimate)

ETHNIC GROUPS
Moldovan and Romanian, 78.2 percent; Ukrainian, 8.4 percent; Russian, 5.8 percent; Gagauz, 4.4 percent; Bulgarian, 1.9 percent; other, 1.3 percent (2004 census)

RELIGION
Eastern Orthodox, 98 percent; Jewish, 1.3 percent; Baptist and others, 0.7 percent (2000 estimate)

LANGUAGES
Moldovan, Romanian, Russian, Gagauz

NATIONAL HOLIDAY
Independence Day: August 27

TIME LINE

IN MOLDOVA	IN THE WORLD
A.D. 1500–1600 Principality of Moldova stretches roughly between Carpathian Mountains and Dniester River.	**1530** Beginning of transatlantic slave trade organized by the Portuguese in Africa
1700–1800 Moldovan territory disputed by several powers, with the Ottoman Empire and Russia as the main rivals.	
	1789–99 The French Revolution
1812 Treaty of Bucharest grants Russia control of eastern Moldova and the Ottoman Empire western Moldova.	
1878 Ottomans recognize independence of Romanian state including western Moldova.	**1869** The Suez Canal is opened. **1914** World War I begins.
1918 Bessarabia declares independence.	**1918** Bolshevik Revolution in Russia
1920 Treaty of Paris recognizes union of Bessarabia with Romania. The Bolsheviks do not.	
1924 Moldovan Autonomous Soviet Socialist Republic established east of the Dniester River within Ukraine	
1939 Romania carved up in pact between Hitler's Germany and Stalin's USSR. Bessarabia goes to the USSR.	**1939** World War II begins.
1940 Russia annexes Bessarabia and combines it with most of the Moldovan Autonomous Soviet Socialist Republic to form Moldavian Soviet Socialist Republic.	
1941–45 Following Nazi attack on USSR, a Romanian puppet regime is installed in Moldavian SSR but driven out shortly before the end of the war when the Soviet Union regains control.	**1945** The United States drops atomic bombs on Hiroshima and Nagasaki. World War II ends.
1986 Resurgence of Moldovan nationalism.	**1986** Era of "openness" introduced in the Soviet Union by Mikhail Gorbachev; nuclear power disaster at Chernobyl in Ukraine
1989 Romanian is reinstated as the official language. The Latin script is adopted to replace the Cyrillic script.	**1991** Breakup of the Soviet Union

IN MOLDOVA	IN THE WORLD

1990

Moldova declares its sovereignty. The Gagauz people declare independence, followed by those in Transnistria. The central power in Moldova annuls these declarations.

1991

Moldova declares its independence.

1992

Moldova becomes a member of the United Nations.

1993

The leu is introduced to replace the ruble.

1994

A new constitution proclaims Moldova's neutrality, grants special autonomy status to the Transnistria and Gagauz regions, and declares Moldovan to be the official language.

1996

Petru Lucinschi is elected president

1997

Hong Kong is returned to China.

1999

OSCE summit sets end of 2002 as deadline for withdrawal of Russian troops and ammunition from Transnistria.

2001

Communist Vladimir Voronin is elected president.

2001

Terrorists crash planes in New York, Washington, D.C., and Pennsylvania.

2002

Plans to make Russian an official language spark mass protests. Deadline for withdrawal of Russian weapons from Transnistria extended.

2003

War in Iraq begins.

2004

Russia says it will complete withdrawal of its forces from Transnistria only when a solution to the conflict is reached.

2005

Communist Party tops poll in elections and returns Vladimir Voronin as president.

2006

Russian gas giant Gazprom cuts off supplies when Moldova refuses to pay double the previous price. Transnistria referendum vote backs independence from Moldova and a plan to eventually become part of Russia.

2008

The first black president of the United States, Barack Obama, is elected.

2009

Ruling Communists declared winners of disputed election. Result triggers violent protests. Voronin resigns as president and is succeeded by Mihai Ghimpu on an acting basis until the election of a new head of state.

GLOSSARY

Agrarian Democratic Party
One of the main political parties in Moldova, led by former Communists.

baklava
A Turkish pastry with crushed pistachios or almonds.

borscht
A Ukrainian national dish that has become a Moldovan favorite.

brinza (BRIHN-zah)
Sheep-milk cheese cured in brine.

ciorba (CHOR-ba)
A sour-tasting Moldovan soup.

Commonwealth of Independent States (CIS)
An alliance consisting of former Soviet republics formed after the fall of the Soviet Union.

Gagauz
A Christian Turkic minority in Moldova.

glasnost
The policy of a more open, consultative government.

gross domestic product (GDP)
The total monetary value of goods and services produced in a country in one year.

International Monetary Fund (IMF)
An international organization that promotes stability in the world's currencies and maintains a fund pool from which member nations can draw.

mamaliga (mah-me-LI-ga)
The national dish of Moldova, made of corn.

mititei (me-tee-TAY)
A traditional dish consisting of grilled meatballs.

North Atlantic Treaty Organization (NATO)
An organization formed for the purpose of collective defense against aggression.

perestroika
The policy of reforming the economic and political system.

placinte (pla-CHIN-te)
A Moldovan turnover.

Union of the Soviet Socialist Republics (USSR)
Official name of the former Soviet Union.

United Nations (UN)
An international organization formed to promote international peace, security, and cooperation.

FOR FURTHER INFORMATION

BOOKS

Ciscel, Matthew H. *The Language of the Moldovans.* Lanham, MD: Lexington Books, 2007.

Hegarty, Thomas, *Moldova* (Postcommunist States and Nations). New York: Routledge, 2003.

Henighan, Stephan. *Lost Province: Adventures in a Moldovan Family.* Totnes, Devon, England: Prospect Books, 2002.

Weiner, Eric. *The Geography of Bliss: One Grump's Search for the Happiest Places in the World.* New York: Hachette Book Group, 2008.

Zlatova, Y and V. Kotelnikov. *Across Moldova.* Honolulu: University Press of the Pacific, 2002.

FILMS

Cea Mai Bun Dintre Lumi Sau Simpla Zi Toamna (The Best of the Worlds). Directed by Sergiu Prodan. Freedom Film Distributors, 1990.

Russian Folk Song and Dance. Kultur Video, 2008.

Ultimul Rol (The Ultimate Role). Directed by Stefan Bulicanu. Freedom Film Distributors, 1999.

MUSIC

Nicolae Bretan: Golem and Arald. Various artists. Nimbus Records, 1995.

Sacred Songs from Moldovia. Ilona Nyisztor. Passion Music, 2006.

Sound the Deep Waters. Izolda. Folk Nouveau Music, 2003.

BIBLIOGRAPHY

BOOKS

Abel, Elie. *The Shattered Bloc*. Boston: Houghton Mifflin Co., 1990.

Dinu, A and M. Rowntree. *Environmental Resources and Constraints in the Former Soviet Republics*. Boulder: Westview Press, 1995.

Dyer, Donald Leroy. *Studies in Moldovan*. Boulder: East European Monographs, 1996.

Kelly, Robert C. *Country Review, Moldova*. Honolulu: Commercial Data International, Inc., 1998.

King, Charles. *Post-Soviet Moldova*. London: Center for Romanian Studies, 1997.

King, Charles. *The Moldovans: Romania, Russia, and the Politics of Culture* (Studies of Nationalities). Stanford: Hoover Institution Press, 2000.

Lerner Geography Department. *Moldova Then and Now*. Minneapolis: Lerner Publications, 1993.

Pryde, Philip. *Environmental Resources and Constraints in the Former Soviet Republics*. Boulder: Westview Press, 1995.

Williams, Nicola and David St. Vincent. *Romania and Moldova Travel Guide*, 1st ed. Victoria, Australia: Lonely Planet Publications, 1998.

WEBSITES

Ask4Geo: Moldova. www.ask4geo.com/moldova.php

BBC News—Country Profile: Moldova. http://news.bbc.co.uk/2/hi/europe/country_profiles/3038982.stm

Encyclopedia Britannica. www.britannica.com

Encyclopedia of the Nations. www.nationsencyclopedia.com/

Every Culture: Moldova. www.everyculture.com/Ma-Ni/Moldova.html

ICE Case Studies: Transnistria-Moldova Conflict. www1.american.edu/ted/ice/moldova.htm

Interlic: Hottest News from Moldova. http://en.interlic.md

Kommersant. www.kommersant.com/t699294/r_2/n_16/Russia_Assured_Moldova_an_Economic_Slump/

Moldova.org. http://docs.moldova.org

Mongabay.com: Moldova—Economy. www.mongabay.com/reference/country_studies/moldova/ECONOMY.html

Nation-by-Nation: Economy—Moldova. www.historycentral.com/NationbyNation/Moldova/Economy.html

Radio Free Europe Radio Liberty. www.rferl.org

Religioscope. www.religioscope.com/articles/2002/012_regmoldova.htm

Republic of Moldova. www.moldova.md/en/start/

INDEX

INDEX